More advance praise for *They Better Call Me Sugar*

"*They Better Call Me Sugar* is fabulous—so infinitely readable and engaging. Sugar Rodgers is such a clear-eyed and thoughtful writer and a huge inspiration. There are so many young people I can't wait to give this book to."
—Jacqueline Woodson, author of *Brown Girl Dreaming*, former National Ambassador for Young People's Literature

"Sugar Rodgers's story will be inspirational not only for young girls, not only for young athletes, but for everyone. You never know the mountains people have to climb to reach the level of success they have achieved."
—Etan Thomas, former NBA player, author of *We Matter: Athletes and Activism*

"Having had the privilege of playing and working with Sugar Rodgers, I've been blessed with a front row seat to watch her grow into the woman she is today. My hope and prayer is that everyone, both young and old, gets an opportunity to read this book and let Sugar—the athlete, the woman, the survivor—have as much of an impact on their lives as she has had on mine."
—Swin Cash, three-time WNBA champion, VP of Basketball Operations with the New Orleans Pelicans

"It would be too easy to say that Sugar Rodgers's memoir is a slam dunk. It's more than that—it's a three-pointer from deep. If you want to know what it takes to shoot for your dreams in sports and in life, read this book."
—C.J. Farley, author of *Around Harvard Square*

SUGAR RODGERS is a professional basketball player currently starring in the WNBA for the Las Vegas Aces. She honed her skills as a young girl growing up in Suffolk, VA, by shooting hoops with neighborhood drug dealers before eventually being recruited by the Georgetown Hoyas, making her the first person in her family to attend college. She graduated Georgetown as the leading scorer of all time, and was drafted by the Minnesota Lynx in 2013. She also played several seasons with the New York Liberty before being traded to Las Vegas in 2019. She was named to the WNBA All-Star team for her 2017 season with the New York Liberty.

THEY BETTER CALL ME

SUGAR

MY JOURNEY FROM THE HOOD TO THE HARDWOOD

SUGAR RODGERS

Published by Akashic Books
©2021 Ta'Shauna "Sugar" Rodgers

Paperback ISBN: 978-1-61775-929-1
Hardcover ISBN: 978-1-63614-013-1
Library of Congress Control Number: 2020948041

Black Sheep
c/o Akashic Books
Brooklyn, New York
Twitter: @AkashicBooks
Facebook: AkashicBooks
E-mail: info@akashicbooks.com
Website: www.akashicbooks.com

Mom, this book is for you! Your soul can rest in peace knowing that I am at peace.

TABLE OF CONTENTS

Introduction   11

Chapter 1: Williamstown   15

Chapter 2: Tomboy   25

Chapter 3: Second Grade   29

Chapter 4: Golf   35

Chapter 5: Tiger Woods and California   45

Chapter 6: My First Jail Visit   51

Chapter 7: Football   57

Chapter 8: Toe-to-Toe with a Drug Dealer   65

Chapter 9: My First Basketball Team   71

Chapter 10: City League Basketball   77

Chapter 11: The Bust   83

Chapter 12: The Tournament   93

Chapter 13: The Funeral   99

Chapter 14: DD Bug   103

Chapter 15: Life at Coach Betty's House   105

Chapter 16: Aunt Linda 113

Chapter 17: Boo Williams 119

Chapter 18: Getting Recruited 129

Chapter 19: Powder Puff 133

Chapter 20: Senior Prom 139

Chapter 21: Georgetown Hoyas 143

Chapter 22: Scooter 149

Chapter 23: Freshman Year 153

Chapter 24: Dad 159

Chapter 25: Senior Year 163

Chapter 26: Preparing for the Pros 167

Chapter 27: Draft Day 169

Chapter 28: Minnesota Lynx 175

Chapter 29: Living the Dream 179

Chapter 30: Dream Big 183

Chapter 31: Self-Talk and Positivity 185

Acknowledgments 191

INTRODUCTION

I'M WRITING THIS BOOK TO SHARE MY STORY, to tell about the challenges I've had to face so far in my life— the various experiences I've been through, and the roadblocks that I've stumbled on during my journey towards a successful life. A life that has rewarded my hard work—currently, I play in the Women's National Basketball Association. We won the championship in 2013 when I was with the Minnesota Lynx, and during my time playing with the New York Liberty, I was an All-Star and won the Sixth Woman of the Year Award in 2017. As I finished writing this book, my current team, the Las Vegas Aces, had just made it to the 2020 WNBA Finals, which were held in a "bubble" due to the Covid-19 pandemic. I am also attending Georgetown University's master's program in Sports Industry Management.

It wasn't always clear that my life would go in such a positive direction. Growing up, I was often forced to figure things out on my own. But I was also lucky enough to have people in my life whom I could get advice and guidance from—people who helped me along the way, and still do to this day. I'm hoping that by sharing my own story, it will help others who might be struggling.

Life, as I've learned sometimes the hard way, will always include obstacles, moments of defeat, but learning how to overcome those obstacles will just make you appreciate your moments of success more. It's important to enjoy your life, to figure out what makes you happy no matter how difficult a time you might be going through. It's important to never give up on yourself. There are lessons learned in every situation, whether you succeed or fail.

My life began with a purpose, though when I was young, I never really understood what that purpose was. I grew up surrounded by drugs and violence in an area with many single-parent households. Amid all of this, I was also surrounded by sports. And despite all the negativity around me, I had my mother to advise and guide me. She always said, "Do your best," and with all the knowledge she shared with me, I was determined to do just that.

My advice to others is that in spite of what you may face in life, you shouldn't lose sight of your goals and dreams. People won't always agree with those goals and dreams, but that's why they are yours. You have to stick with them no matter how hard things get. Find something that you are passionate about, something that drives you, whether it's education, sports, or maybe even politics. Sometimes it may seem like the whole world is against you. In those dark moments, you have to keep believing in yourself and remain positive.

Dreams do come true. But for this to happen, you have to believe in yourself, do your schoolwork, and work hard—even when no one is watching. Stars are stars because they work hard even when the lights are not on.

Be watchful in your everyday struggles and pay attention to the things going on around you. In school, teachers focus on subjects like math, science, history, English, and physical education, and these are certainly important. But there are many other important lessons too, basics that you learn in your daily life.

While the main readers I'm hoping to reach are the young ones, I also have a few words of advice to adults: In this world we call life, it's crucial to remember that the children are our future; and it's up to adults to offer advice, guidance, inspiration, and support along the way—to give children the confidence and skills they need in order to overcome any obstacles they may face. They can overcome obstacles as long as they never stop believing.

CHAPTER 1

WILLIAMSTOWN

::

DECEMBER 8, 1989, WAS ONE OF the coldest days of the year. In the midst of a snowstorm, my mother went into labor with me. She knew it would be nearly impossible for an ambulance to reach her in the storm, so she did her best to deal with the painful contractions, which kept coming more and more frequently. Throughout this, surrounded by friends, family, and even some customers, my mother continued to serve alcohol at the place we called the Shot House, where Canadian Mist was fifty cents a shot and gin shots were a dollar. Her customers that night had no idea what a surprise they were in for.

Though she was scared to push before the ambulance arrived, eventually my mother could not hold back any longer. So she went to her bedroom, lay down on the bed, and proceeded to push. Everyone at the Shot House was anxious—terrified, in fact. You would have thought that giving birth would be a moment of happiness, but my mother was startled when she didn't hear her baby crying. Little did she know that the umbilical cord was wrapped around my throat. My mother's friend Lee Claire was thankfully able to unwrap the cord and save my life.

After two hours of a painful labor and a complicated birth, my mother was blessed with a healthy baby girl. But there was a surprising twist—throughout her entire pregnancy, my mother believed she was having a boy. A boy she planned to name Ty'Shawn Rodgers. My mother was stunned to find out she'd given birth to a girl, and she decided to name me Ta'Shauna. However, my uncle and mother gave that baby girl a nickname that people would come to know and love: Sugar.

At the age of forty-two, my mother needed to adjust to having a newborn in her life again. She was also raising my older brother, DeShawn, known as DD Bug, who was five at the time, and helping out my older sister, Sharon, who already had her own daughter and two young sons.

Though my mother's official name was Barbara Mae Rodgers, everyone called her Bob Mae. Those who knew Bob Mae knew that she was a jack of all trades. She sold everything—she was the best candy lady on the block. She had everything from chewies to chips, but Kool-Aid and snowballs were her specialties. Her Kool-Aid was always on point—not too sweet, not too sour.

But during the summer, it was all about her snowballs, which were delicious. She had the block jumping with those. Snowballs were always fifty cents apiece, and my mother's weren't those inferior kind that you could suck the juice out of like you got other places in the hood. These were snowballs that you took and flipped over with your hand, after you licked your fingers, then bit into with your front teeth. After you were done eating the ice, you'd drink the juice out of the bottom of the cup. There were plenty of ways to eat a snowball, but if you ate my mother's with your fingers, everyone would know you'd had one—your fingers would be the color of the snowball for the rest of the day.

So my mother was the candy lady, but that wasn't all. She was the neighborhood caretaker and late at night, she was the woman with the Shot House. While some might have viewed the Shot House as simply a place were people got drunk, ate chicken, and partied, a place where some nights ended in violence, Bob Mae strived to bring people together to reminisce, to laugh, and to enjoy each other's company. My mother had a big heart and despite the difficulties we faced, I always knew I was loved.

I remember my early childhood as some of the best years of my life; I didn't have a care in the world. I grew up in Suffolk, Virginia, in a neighborhood called Williamstown. It wasn't just any old neighborhood— it was full of gangs, drug dealers, and poverty. Most people would refer to it as a ghetto, but for me, it was home. I lived there with my mother, older brother, older niece, and often two older nephews—my sister Sharon's kids.

Bob Mae was basically the mother of the neighborhood and she knew what was going on throughout the whole city. She got so much love and respect from everybody. While male figures came in and out of our lives over the years, the one constant was our mother. She raised us to be the best we could be. She was a single parent who worked two jobs and lived on food stamps to make ends meet. Despite these difficulties, she always put food on the table and clothes on our backs. During my childhood, I felt like we were living the good life, despite being poor.

We all lived in a one-story house that had three bedrooms, one bathroom, a living room, dining room, and kitchen. The house was the oldest one on the block, having been passed down from generation to generation. From the outside, it looked like you could literally push it over. The paint was chipping off the walls and it had a tin roof. The ceilings leaked and the floors were caving in all over, but we didn't mind much. From time to time, we would try to patch things up, though that only lasted so long. And while the house had many problems, it also held so many of our memories—it was a good home to my family.

One thing, however, that made the place a bit hard to live in at times was that my mother was a hoarder. When I was a kid, I never paid too much attention to the mounds of junk piled up everywhere. I just stepped around or on it like it wasn't even there. I never wanted any of my friends to come to the house, though, because I was embarrassed.

My mother just couldn't help herself. She would never throw anything away. Nearly every Saturday, she and her girlfriends would go to yard sales and buy stuff that we didn't need and would never use. So the inside of our house looked almost like a landfill.

The mess certainly didn't help with our cockroach problem. It was common for me to pour myself a bowl of cereal, add in the milk, and find a roach floating at the top. Plenty of days I would open the refrigerator door to find a dead roach lying right beside what I was about to eat. If the roach wasn't *on* the actual food, I was okay. If it was on the wrapper, I would pluck or blow it off. Sometimes, I would throw the roaches on top of the kerosene heater and watch them die—hoping if I taught one a lesson they would all go away. (We didn't have central heating, so we relied on three heaters and a kitchen stove to keep us warm. Because of this, my clothes always smelled like kerosene.) But after a while, I stopped trying to the kill them; they outnumbered me anyway.

As bad as they were, I would take the roaches any day over the fleas. I remember one time it was so bad, I had to wear long socks in the house because we had fleas from the two dogs Sharon left us when she got locked up. You would never catch me on the floor, just lying down watching TV like a normal kid. Them fleas would tear me up, and we didn't get rid of them until the dogs passed away. I swear, I'd rather have a crackhead in my house than roaches and fleas.

My father was retired from the military and lived with his wife in the suburbs. Unless he was sick or had other obligations, he would visit us pretty much every day. I was always torn when he left our house to go home to his other family. Part of me wanted him to stay, but I started to realize he only stayed over when he was too drunk to go home.

"Sugar," he'd say, his words coming out a bit slurred, "come here. You know I love you, right?"

I'd look over at him like, *Duh, you* better *love me*.

I could smell the alcohol on his breath. In fact, it would smell like he had taken a bath in it, the fumes were so strong. When he was drunk, it felt to me like he wasn't even my dad but some stranger who came around from time to time. I'd watch him stumble around the house and I'd think, *Who is this guy? Why does he drink so much? Where is my dad? I don't like this guy.*

But I was also scared to leave him alone because I thought he might hurt himself. So I'd stay by his side while he told me stories about his past—stories he never would have shared with me when he was sober. I knew I could have asked him anything on those days, but I mostly kept quiet. Although he looked like my dad, this person wasn't him.

For the majority of my childhood, my sister Sharon ran the streets, and her children were not her first priority—the street was her life. She sold drugs not only in my neighborhood but up and down the East Coast. It was normal for her to disappear for weeks at a time, leaving her children with our mom or at her house, knowing my mother would look after them. Sharon would call every so often to check up on them. Her children's baby daddy wasn't around like a father should be, and she knew our mother was someone she could depend on.

Whenever my sister did show up, she would shower us with gifts, making sure we had the hottest shoes, clothes, and whatever else we asked for. I looked forward to her visits as I knew she'd always arrive with something new for me.

One time, she took us to Kings Dominion in Doswell, Virginia. It was the first time I'd ever been to an amusement park, and I loved it. She would also take us to Maryland to see my mother's sister. I never really knew why we were visiting Aunt Amanda, but it was still fun, and I enjoyed it.

When Sharon was around, I loved staying with her. We could do whatever we wanted at her place. When I was young she lived close enough to us that I could ride my bike or walk to her apartment, but eventually she moved to Newport News, and the only way to get there was by car. Until one day she got caught dealing again—her so-called best friend set her up—and since it wasn't her first offense, she was sentenced to ten years in prison.

It was around Easter 1998, and I recall my mother telling her, "Don't go to your house. Come straight here, Sharon." From time to time, my mother would have these weird feelings, and when she had them, something bad always happened. Unfortunately, my sister did the opposite of what my mother said and went home. As soon she walked through the door, the feds busted in right behind her. My mother got a phone call from someone who told her something was going on at Sharon's house. My mother, my niece, and I knew we had to get to Newport News as fast as possible to see what was going on.

It was really early, and I was barely awake. I threw on some sweats and my coat over my shorts and T-shirt, while my mother and niece got ready as well. Once in the car, I started in on the chips, soda, and whatever other junk was there in the backseat, then quickly fell back to sleep.

The sound of my niece crying woke me. Both she and my mother had jumped out of the car as soon as we'd arrived at Sharon's, and they were so focused on what was going on that they'd left me in the car. I lay there for a moment on my back looking up at the roof. I could see blue and red lights flashing outside, and I popped up to see what was going on, staying down low enough so I could look out the window but no one could see me.

What I witnessed was something out of a gangster movie. There were police everywhere. My niece was crying and screaming, "Don't take my mother!" Bob Mae just stood there watching as two cops escorted my handcuffed sister out to their vehicle. It was the first time I'd ever seen my sister in handcuffs. I knew bad people went to jail, but my sister wasn't bad! I adored her and so did everyone else—everyone besides the police.

CHAPTER 2

TOMBOY

ONCE I STARTED SCHOOL AND WAS OLD ENOUGH to hang out, I ran the streets with my friends. For whatever reason, nearly all of them were boys, so I adopted the mentality of a tomboy. I began to feel like I could do things just as well as the boys could; therefore, I played golf, football, and marbles all day, every day. I even fixed bikes and worked on motor scooters. Despite this, my mother always said that tomboys still needed to get their hair done. As a kid, I didn't agree with her, because I hated it. A hairstyle for me was rocking cornrows.

My niece Ebony, known as Kakie, who was older than me, didn't like me running around like a little boy. She would say, "I hope you grow out of this tomboy thing. I hope you don't be gay." But she also knew that I never liked getting my hair done, so she would do four or five cornrows that would stay in my hair until they almost dreaded up. My mother and Kakie got into plenty of arguments over my hair, and in her anger, my niece would hurt my head on purpose. She would braid it tight, push my head hard from side to side, and say mean things like, "Keep your head still—dang, that's why I don't like doing your stupid hair." I loved my niece but I hated her when it was time to get my hair done.

My mother made me wear girlie clothes to school, but of course I would always return home with grass in my hair and dirt stains all over. Basketball shorts and T-shirts were so comfortable that every day after school I would change into them before grabbing my basketball to go to the side of my house where I had my basketball goal. We couldn't afford a brand-new goal but my brother had bought one for cheap from this white guy who lived down the street. It had a black pole with a square wooden backboard; we could only get it to stand up by putting center blocks with tires on top of the part that was meant to be filled with water. The rim was bent, but our mother gave us money to buy another one for around fifteen dollars at Walmart.

At first, my brother would put it back together for me when it fell down, but eventually he stopped after my friends and I kept dunking on it. Finally, after several tries, my friends and I figured out how to put it together on our own. Very soon, my basketball goal became *the* hangout spot for everybody in the neighborhood, including small kids, drug dealers, parents, and others. It seemed as if that goal brought my neighborhood together. The other kids and I would gather around it to laugh, joke, bet money, and, of course, play basketball. Every day it seemed as if there was a parade on my street because so many people were hanging out around that goal.

Before long, crowds of people started attracting unnecessary attention—attention that tried to prevent us from having a good time. The police always wanted to take the goal away. When I was growing up in Williamstown, the police (or, as they were typically referred to: *one time, pigs, five-o, po-po*) were considered to be the bad guys in my neighborhood, because in our eyes, they always ruined the fun.

For example, one day an officer told us that we had to turn my goal around so it didn't face the curb. But as children, who listens to the police when you are having fun doing something you've been doing after school every day for weeks? We were sick of the cops coming around and harassing us just for playing basketball in the street, so we didn't stop. And it's not like we had a park to play in. So we said, "Fuck the police," and continued playing in the street. Eventually, a police truck came to confiscate the goal.

I ran into the house to get my mother.

"The fucking police is trying to take our basketball goal, and we didn't do nothing wrong," I told her.

My mother stopped what she was doing and went outside to talk to the cops. "What's the problem, officer?" she asked politely.

The officer responded, "Well, ma'am, we asked the kids to turn the goal the other way, but they didn't listen. We warned them plenty of times to turn it around, and the kids just kept ignoring us. So we're here to take the goal down to headquarters. You can come and pick it up from the station, ma'am."

My mother was calm when she said, "If y'all want them to stay out of the street, build them a park where they can play."

I nodded my head as if to say, *Yeah, build us a damn park!*

The police took the goal, but my mother did go downtown and pick it up from the station. She soon returned home with it and we were back in action. The fact is, that goal was the reason why a lot of us stayed out of trouble after school, and years later that goal would change my life.

CHAPTER 3

SECOND GRADE

SECOND GRADE WAS NO FUN FOR ME. My grades weren't good and my dad and mom did not play when it came to school, especially my dad. Every day after school, I would sit at the table with him and do my homework. Most afternoons, one of my friends from the neighborhood would come by to try and get me to go out and play.

While I sat there struggling over my school assignments, I'd hear a knock at our door.

"Who is it?" my mother would call out.

"It's Trell. Can Sugar come outside?"

"Sugar's not coming out right now, Trell. Maybe later, but not right now."

All I wanted to do was go outside with my friends! But no, I had to stay inside and do my stupid homework.

I was good at every subject in school except for reading. I was struggling to read at my grade level, and my mom and dad couldn't figure out why. I would come home with a D in reading on every progress report.

So after we finished my homework, we would stay at that table doing extra reading and writing assignments. My dad was especially big on *penmanship*, as he called it. But I still struggled with reading and I dreaded having to read aloud in school.

"Who wants to read this sentence?" our teacher asked the class one morning. Nearly all my classmates raised their hands.

"TaShauna!" called the teacher. I sat there thinking, *I didn't raise my hand, so why the hell is she calling on me?* Plus, I never responded when people called me by my government name, so I sat there silently.

"Sugar! Can you read the next sentence in the book?"

I didn't want to do it, but I knew I had to try.

To many of my classmates, the sentence was simple: *We will go to Grandmother's house for cookies.* But that same sentence was different in my mind. It wasn't simple. Nonetheless I tried, and slowly stumbled through it: "We . . . will . . . go . . . to . . . Grand . . . mother haus—"

"House," my teacher corrected.

"For," I continued, "cokies."

"Cookies," my teacher corrected again.

I remember feeling embarrassed, nervous, sweaty, stumbling over words; I vowed to myself that no matter how many times she called on me, I would never read aloud again. I didn't even care how much trouble I might get into with my parents.

It seemed like every day after that, my teacher would call on me to read. But I kept refusing and eventually she would call on the next kid. Nearly every day I had a letter in my folder to give to my mom and dad, and most of the time my teacher also called my parents to let them know I was still refusing to read aloud. For the majority of second grade, I would get my ass whooped after school.

It finally got so bad, it started to affect *all* my grades, even in gym. My mom knew how much I loved gym, and knew something needed to be done. So the next time my teacher called, they arranged a meeting at the school.

No one told me what was discussed, but the next day when it was time to read aloud, the teacher didn't call on me. Instead, another teacher came in and took me out of the class. I was confused and a little nervous.

"You're not in trouble," the new teacher told me. "From now on, during reading you will be coming with me."

I still didn't know what was going on, but if it got me out of reading, I was down.

We finally got to his classroom after stopping and picking up a few more kids along the way. Everybody rushed to their seats—I just stood there, unsure of what to do.

"TaShauna, you can sit here."

"I don't go by TaShauna," I told him.

"Okay. So what should I call you?"

"Sugar."

"Sugar it is! So, Sugar, you will be sitting here from now on."

I took my seat and finally had the courage to ask, "Why am I here?"

He explained that instead of reading aloud with my classmates, I would come to his classroom and do reading assignments on a computer. "I'll give you a pair of headphones, and the computer will read the assignments for you."

As he set up my workstation, I couldn't help but think to myself that only slow kids were taken out of class, and I wasn't slow.

But it turned out that doing the assignments on the computer really helped. In fact, reading was finally *fun*. After going to that class for the remainder of the year, all of my grades started to improve.

However, my mom and dad were still concerned. So they had another school meeting at the end of the term, and afterward they told me that I wouldn't be going on to the third grade the following year. Even though my work had improved enough to just barely pass second grade, my parents didn't think it was a good idea to promote me.

"If we let you go to the third grade next year, you will just keep struggling and the situation will only get worse," my mother explained.

Truthfully, I really didn't understand their decision, especially since my grades had improved. I just knew my friends were all going on to third grade and I would probably get picked on because I'd failed second grade. But the decision was made and I had to repeat second grade.

CHAPTER 4

GOLF

I NEVER VIEWED MYSELF AS ATHLETIC, until age ten when I knocked out a church window with a golf ball that I hit from across a field. The golf club belonged to a kid in my neighborhood, and it seemed as if I had played almost every sport you could think of at that point except golf. After lying about the window to everybody because I was afraid of getting in trouble, word got back to a local golf coach, who approached me about joining his team. I was happy, yet baffled when he asked because I'd always thought of golf as a white person's sport.

I can remember that day like it was yesterday—running to my house and asking my mother if I could try out for the golf team.

My mother looked at me like, *Are you serious?* Then she asked me who was coaching the team, and I said, "Some guy named Mr. Hunt."

Despite her initial reaction, my mother was interested because her longtime friend, Mr. Ben, who lived up the road, had a son who played golf. She also knew it would help keep me out of trouble and off the streets. I knew Lil Ben (Mr. Ben's son) pretty well. We were in the same class at school and would often hang out. So my mother decided to let me give it a try.

The first day of practice with the Southeastern Junior Golf Association, I took the club and knocked the ball straight down the driving range; everybody was impressed. Soon after, my mother bought me some nice khakis and a red polo shirt she found at the local dollar store. We stayed balling on a budget. Mr. Hunt gave me a set of ugly golf clubs and bag the very same day. The clubs meant that I had made the team. I was so excited, and when I took the clubs home, I wouldn't let anybody touch them. A few weeks later everybody in the neighborhood was signing up to join the golf team, including my siblings.

There were three levels: beginner, intermediate, and advanced. I started out with the beginner group, but within a couple of weeks, I had learned the basics of golf: putting and chipping, the etiquette and rules. I had to wear the khakis and red polo shirt, and my mother had to provide the socks and shoes. Before she bought them, however, she made sure I was really into the sport, since she didn't want to waste her money.

Moving up to intermediate was fun because my older siblings were still in the beginner's group. Although I was the youngest in age, I was the oldest in status when it came to the golf course. Being on an intermediate level meant I spent a lot of time at the driving range working on my swing, hitting out of the sand, and playing on the one-hole practice course. I knew golf was a sport that I would enjoy because it was nothing like my neighborhood. The golf course was quiet and peaceful; it was a place where I could relax. A place where I didn't have to worry about life, and could simply live it while doing something I loved.

It only took me another couple of months to move up to the advanced group. Now it was my turn to hit the course, something I'd dreamed of since I'd gotten my clubs. Just a few days before I stepped foot on the course, I received a better set of clubs and bag.

Next up for me was my very first golf tournament at Portsmouth City Park. It was cold out and I shivered while waiting for my turn, standing there in my nicely pressed khakis with my polo underneath a red coat my mother had gotten from a coat drive. I was nervous when it was my turn, but I grabbed a tee and ball and moved forward with my driver in the other hand. I placed the ball on the tee and took a couple of practice swings before hitting the ball into the middle of the fairway.

After we played nine holes, the scores were added

up and the player with the lowest score won. My group included my friend from up the street and some random white girl. I know you're thinking the white girl won, right?

Once they collected all the scores from the other groups, they would post who won on a big board outside, where the parents and players could see. Then the winners were announced over a loud-speaker. Girls were announced first, then the boys. I already knew what place I was in from the score-board, which read: *Sugar Rodgers, 3rd Place.*

I had to go inside to get my trophy and a $50 gift card to the golf club's gift shop. I used it to buy all the socks $50 could afford. I loved the way those socks felt in my hand and I couldn't wait to put them on my feet.

My friend who came in second place won a $100 gift card. I was happy for her, but I was also mad because I hated losing. I was frustrated with myself because I knew if I'd won the tournament I would have received a $150 gift card—just think of all the socks I could have bought with that!

And, you guessed it, the white girl did come in first.

I couldn't wait to get home. I silently cried in the backseat of Mr. Ben's car so no one would see me. But as soon as he dropped me off, I ran into the house weeping so loudly that my mother thought somebody had hurt me. When she saw that I wasn't physically harmed in any way, she went outside to thank Mr. Ben for taking me and collected my golf clubs and third-place trophy from his car. When she came back in, I was in her bedroom lying on her bed in my underwear, still crying. I explained to her that I felt like I'd been cheated.

She said, in her soft tone that made everything seem better, "Honey, it's okay. Third place isn't bad. You just have to work a little harder."

"But Mom, the girl from up the street beat me," I moaned.

"She just had a better day than you, sweetie," she soothed.

From that day on, my mother went to every golf practice and tournament. She was right by my side when I won first for the first time, which happened to be at the very next golf tournament. After that, I won the $150 gift card almost every time. When I did, I would buy more socks.

Before long, I became number one in the state, and I started receiving letters in the mail from university golf teams around the country. There was one person at that time who every young black golfer wanted to meet, and that was Tiger Woods. Tiger was the shit. He was winning all the major tournaments, like the Masters. Black people didn't win shit like that. He was my favorite golfer of all time because he was black and doing it big in what I still thought of as a white person's sport.

And guess what? I got to meet *the* Tiger Woods in person. I was invited to a camp he was holding in Norfolk—one of his first camps in Virginia. I was so excited I couldn't sleep and spent the night before the camp washing my golf clubs and teasing my siblings about getting to meet him. They got to come and *see* him from afar, but since I was on the elite level now I was getting to meet Tiger in person, and something like that made you a star in my hood. A couple of other kids from my area were invited as well, so the morning the camp began we carpooled to Norfolk.

While my siblings all wore khakis and red polo shirts—red was the neighborhood team color—I wore all Nike gear: black shorts, hat, socks, and shirt. There was nothing like wearing Nike back then; it was expensive and we could rarely afford it.

When we arrived, my mother and I joined the rest of the elite golfers who would have the chance to meet and work with Tiger. After checking in, we headed to the driving range where Tiger was giving the lessons. I hit a couple balls while watching him work with some of the other kids from my team.

My mother had schooled me the night before on how to act so I wouldn't embarrass myself, or her. When it was my turn, I politely shook his hand as he introduced himself: "Hi, I'm Tiger Woods."

Duh is what I was thinking to myself, but out loud I said, "Hi, my name is . . ." and then I paused briefly, unsure if I should say Sugar or Ta'Shauna. I decided to use my proper name: "My name is Ta'Shauna Rodgers."

"Nice to meet you," he said.

"Nice to meet you too."

"Show me your swing, Ta'Shana," Tiger said, mispronouncing my name like everyone always did.

So I took a couple of swings and he gave a couple of pointers. And then it was over, just like that.

Now it was time to relax and watch Tiger put on a show with trick shots, chipping, and long drives. Little did I know I was in for a huge surprise that my mother had somehow forgotten to mention. I was going to be in a Tiger Woods Foundation Coca-Cola commercial the next day!!

At this point, I was tired and ready to go home—it had been a long day. But my mother and I wanted to scope out where they would be shooting the commercial, and I had to memorize a few lines that my mother helped me with.

The next day when we went to the commercial shoot, I said my three lines:

"*All I need to do is stay focused and trust myself.*"

"*You can change the world.*"

"*I can do it.*"

And then I was out. They told my mother we would receive a copy of the commercial when it was done. She was so proud of me and bragged all over town about how her baby was in a Tiger Woods commercial. That commercial also helped me with my fifth grade play. There were only four lead speaking roles and I wanted to be one of them. So I brought a copy of the commercial to school and gave it to the drama teacher. My teacher took it home, watched it, and the next day one of those speaking parts was mine, just like that!

I was, of course, excited about having the role, but I didn't actually like speaking in front of a lot of people. It was nothing like the commercial where I just had to say a couple of lines with only a few people watching. It was a Christmas play and I would have to memorize over twenty-two lines. I became so anxious leading up to the performance that at one point I pretended to be sick. When that didn't get me out of the play, I knew I had to focus and learn my lines. Yet again, it was my mother who helped me memorize my lines. She wasn't going to let me embarrass her by forgetting them, but most importantly she wasn't going to let me embarrass myself.

On the day of the play, I had to wear a hat, scarf, and a big Suffolk Steelers coat my mother got from another coat drive. Because it was a Christmas play, we had to act like we were outside in the snow. I was burning up on stage with that big coat on and the heat pumping throughout the building. I spotted my mother and father in the stands smiling proudly at their baby girl on stage. I was glad to see them, but they also made me nervous.

After the play was over, we snapped pictures and then my dad took us out to eat at McDonald's.

CHAPTER 5

TIGER WOODS AND CALIFORNIA

OVER THE NEXT COUPLE OF YEARS, I continued to play golf and eventually I was ranked number one in the state of Virginia.

One day after practice, my coach informed my mom that I'd been invited to play on Tiger Woods's golf team at an international tournament taking place in California. I was super excited. *I* was going to be representing Tiger Woods. My mom was stunned, and on the car ride home she was silent. I sat in the passenger seat, just looking out the window— I'd never been to California; I'd never even been on a plane before!

As soon as we got home, my mom couldn't wait to call everybody she knew to share the news. I ran outside to tell my friends. Some of them used to play golf, but they hadn't lasted very long and often made fun of me for sticking with the game.

"Sugar, it's about time you finished with that white-man sport," said CJ, one of the neighborhood boys, when he saw me in my golf clothes.

Everybody except me busted out laughing.

"Y'all just mad because y'all can't play," I replied.

"Just 'cause you play golf don't make you better than nobody."

"It *does* make me better than you at golf. Duh! And just for y'all's information, I got invited to play on Tiger Woods's team in California."

Well, that certainly shut everyone up for a few seconds.

"Stop lying," CJ said, breaking the silence.

"I'm not lying. You shut up with your ugly self."

"You going to play for the real Tiger Woods?" another kid shouted.

"Yes, the *real* Tiger Woods!"

And all of a sudden, with the news of my connection to a real-life superstar, the teasing stopped. Golf was no longer a white man's game that I was wasting my time with.

"Yo, tell him your homeboy CJ said what's up."

We all laughed, and then spent the rest of the evening running around the neighborhood until the streetlights came on, calling most of us back home.

Later that evening after dinner, my mom and I sat down at the kitchen table to discuss the trip. Almost all my expenses were covered, except for the flights for me and my mom. Of course, I knew that my mom couldn't just drop cash on plane tickets—we didn't have it like that. Plus, she had other responsibilities—

she was the provider for our family. So, she explained, we would have to fundraise to afford the flights.

I wasn't too worried about this. My mom was a hustler; I knew she would come up with the money. And she did just that.

Lil Ben was also invited; they too were able to raise the money. And a couple weeks later we were headed to California. Not only was it my first plane ride, but I was going to miss a full week of school.

We got to the airport early, and after checking in we went to wait by our gate. I took a seat by a window and stared out at the plane we would soon be boarding. It was huge. Much bigger than the planes I'd seen on TV.

"Sugar," my mom said, interrupting my thoughts, "it's time for us to board."

I took my seat next to her and plugged in my headphones to listen to music during the long flight. I'd "borrowed" my brother's portable CD player, and I knew he was going to be mad at me. I'd also taken some of my niece's R&B and hip-hop CDs. I was probably going to get beat up by both of them when I got home. But I didn't care, I was headed to California!

The flight went by pretty quickly, and after we collected our luggage, we took a taxi to the hotel that the team had arranged for us. When we got to the room, there was a welcome package with gear for me. Not just any gear, but *Nike* gear—shirts, hats, shoes. It felt like Christmas. I couldn't wait to wear my new clothes at the tournament.

That night, I laid out my outfit like it was the first day of school. It was a giant event—all the top golfers would be there, and I was one of them.

The next day went by in a blur, and while I ended up losing, the whole experience was dope.

After California, I played in a couple of local tournaments—but the experience wasn't the same. For one thing, my mom stopped going with me. She started sending me with Mr. Ben and I quickly lost my passion for golf. I was winning, but it just wasn't the same without my mom there. I don't know why she stopped going; maybe she was too busy or thought I didn't need her there. I never figured it out, but then again, I never asked her either. I just accepted this change, and with it, my love for the sport started to fade.

While my interest in golf was diminishing, my love of basketball was not. Most days after school, all my friends would come over and we'd play outside my house. Even after the sun went down and all of my friends had gone home, I would stay out there shooting hoops and letting my imagination run wild until my mom called me in . . . or until I heard gunshots and knew it was no longer safe to stay outside.

Usually I'd be on the winning team—narrating like I was a TV sports announcer. *"Sugar Rodgers for three to win the game!"* I'd yell, running around in the street like it was the final moments of a championship game.

I remember this one day, after shouting out my usual, *"Sugar Rodgers for three!"* I shot and missed. I was so angry, I grabbed the rebound and slammed the ball to the ground. Then I kicked it into the street and a car ran over it, bursting it. Even angrier now, I sprinted home, slamming the front door behind me.

"Sugar, don't you slam my damn door like that!" my mom snapped.

"Mom, my ball got ran over so now I can't play on my basketball goal," I said with tears in my eyes.

"I don't have no money to keep spending on basketballs," she responded.

"Mom, please, can you buy me a new basketball? *Pleeeeaase!"*

"Go get my keys. This is the last basketball you getting." She said that every time I needed a new one.

We drove to Walmart and I picked out a new rubbery ball. There is no feeling like getting a new basketball!

CHAPTER 6

MY FIRST JAIL VISIT

IT WAS A BEAUTIFUL FALL WEDNESDAY EVENING and I was going to visit Sharon in jail.

"Sugar, come on!" my mom yelled.

"I'm coming, I'm just looking for my jacket."

"Hurry up!"

I found my jacket stuffed away in my book bag and raced out to the car where my mom and Kakie sat waiting. I hopped into the backseat, excited to see my big sister. I knew it was even more important to Kakie since Sharon was her mom and all, but Kakie got to visit every Wednesday night with my mom. Usually I wasn't allowed to go with them, but for some reason Mom had decided to let me come along this time.

The ride wasn't very far—the jail was right across the street from my elementary school. It kind of looked like an office building, but with tiny windows and barbed wire surrounding it. It was the first time I had visited someone in jail.

We entered the building and I stayed very close to my mom and Kakie. There were a couple police officers behind a wooden desk and we made our way towards them. I was feeling anxious, as I often did around cops.

"Who you here to see?" one of the officers barked at us.

"Sharon Rodgers," my mother said.

"How many people do you have with you?"

"Two."

"Are they under the age of eighteen?"

"Yes."

"ID."

Mom handed the officer her driver's license and he glanced at it before giving her a clipboard. "Sign right here."

Once we were checked in, we sat down and waited. A lady officer stuck her head out of a metal door and started calling out names: "Cassidy Baker, Ana Baker, Diamond Hill, Kendra Holland, Samantha James, Barbara Jordan, Lisa Lee, Rebecca Smith, Yolanda Smith, Lee Wong . . ." She paused and then repeated the names.

As the names were called, people would stand and make their way towards the lady officer. They went through a big metal door with a tiny glass window and disappeared from sight. We were there for what seemed like hours. People came and went, but we remained seated, waiting for them to call my sister's name.

Eventually, the same lady officer came out again

and read from a new list of names: "Mone Alston, Anika Bailey, Jean Butts, Kim Harden, Kay King, Sharon Rodgers, Tonia Scott, Cali Thomas, Meka Williams . . ."

As soon as we heard my sister's name, we stood up and I followed Mom and Kakie through the metal door. We entered a long room with all these ladies in orange jumpsuits sitting behind glass windows. Most of them were smiling.

We kept walking towards the back of the room and I could see Sharon in the distance. She was smiling and waving through the thick glass.

When we got to my sister, my mom sat down and picked up the phone. They each put one hand on either side the glass to make contact. My mom started talking a mile a minute, filling Sharon in on everything that had happened since their last visit.

I was at a loss for words, sitting there looking at all these ladies smiling behind the glass. It was like they were animals in a zoo. Locked up with officers pacing back and forth on their side of the glass. While I knew plenty of people who'd been thrown in jail, I'd never really thought about what that meant.

Once my mom finished talking, she handed the phone to Kakie. Mom, Kakie, and Sharon were all smiling from ear to ear, laughing even. I was still glancing around, somewhat stunned, wondering what had landed all these ladies behind bars. Though my sister had spent time in jail before, in my experience it was usually the men who ended up in jail—at least that was typically the case in my neighborhood. I was zoned out, troubled by the fact that these beautiful ladies were being treated like caged animals.

"Sugar!" Kakie shouted as she passed me the phone, jerking me back to reality. I put the phone to my ear and placed my hand on the window. Like she'd done with my mom and Kakie, Sharon put her hand on her side of the window. I couldn't feel nothing but cold glass. I guess it was the *thought* of touching her that counted.

"Sugar, you grown since the last time I seen you! How's everything going? How's school? How's golf?"

I held the phone tightly in my hand, pressing it against my ear. "Everything is good. I'm making good grades. Golf is good," I replied in a trembling voice.

"That's great to hear," Sharon said with a big smile on her face.

But before I could continue, Kakie snatched the phone from me. "Guess what, Mom?" she yelled into the phone, then started in on some neighborhood gossip.

I just sat there staring at my sister through the glass. When an officer came in and announced, "Twenty minutes left!" Kakie handed the phone back to my mom. While my mom and Sharon continued catching up, I kept looking around at all the ladies with their name tags sitting behind those glass windows smiling; name tags that included out-of-focus photos along with their prisoner numbers. I'd seen things like this in movies and on TV, and plenty of my friends had talked about the times they'd visited people in jail. But to actually be there was different. My big sister was in jail and I had no idea when she might be coming home.

"Ten minutes!" the lady officer called out.

I turned my attention back to my sister; now she was getting choked up. Kakie and Mom had tears in their eyes too, and I realized my own eyes had started to water. I was overwhelmed with emotion, plus I didn't like to see my mom cry—that always made me cry as well.

"Why y'all crying?" I asked my mom, tears streaming down my face.

While still holding the phone so Sharon could hear, Mom explained: "There's nothing like your child having her freedom. And that's what makes it so hard to see her locked up like this because of a mistake she made. And a mistake *was* made," she went on, glancing sternly at Sharon, before turning back to me and Kakie, "but y'all better not follow in the same footsteps, you understand me?" I could hear the pain in her voice, as well as the forcefulness.

My sister just started weeping, and while I understood what Mom was saying, I didn't quite understand why she was telling me this at such a young age.

My mother passed the phone to me one last time so I could say my goodbye.

"I love you," Sharon said through the phone.

"I love you too!" I exclaimed.

I passed the phone to Kakie and she said the same thing with tears still running down her face.

And just like that the visit was over. On our way out we could see Sharon in the distance blowing kisses through the glass, mouthing, *I love y'all!* She kept smiling the whole time, even with tears flowing down her cheeks, and she watched us as we walked out of the room and into freedom.

"Can I go with you again next week?" I asked my mom as soon as we were back in the car.

"We shall see," she responded in her cheerful voice.

On the car ride home all I could do was imagine what life was like behind that glass.

CHAPTER 7

FOOTBALL

I LIKED PLAYING FOOTBALL TOO, because I could take out my anger on the neighborhood field. Naturally, I was the only girl playing football with the boys. Sometimes my brother DD Bug would play with us. He had signed up for the Suffolk Steelers, but he wasn't allowed to play because he couldn't make the weight. He was a little too big for his age. We had fun making sure somebody from each team was the same size and age so they could guard each other. I'll never forget those games.

Down . . . set . . . hut one . . . hut two . . . hike! And I was off—tackling, slamming the boys to the ground. I was rough. I would hurt them and make them cry. And I enjoyed this—it made me feel like I had the block on lock.

Down . . . set . . . hut one . . . hike! I remember one game when my cousin, who was playing on the other team, caught the ball and started running wild. As I sprinted over to tackle him, he stiff-armed me. I fell to the ground and watched as my teammates chased after him, but he had already scored the touchdown.

When I stood up, my head was spinning and it felt like my nose was running. I wiped my nose on my shirt and realized he had hit me so hard he'd given me a bloody nose. It hurt like crazy, but I didn't let myself cry in public. In my hood, whenever someone cried they'd be teased for days.

One of my friends noticed my bloody nose and asked, "You okay, Sugar?"

"I'm okay," I said. "I'm gonna run home and clean my nose and change my shirt. I'll be back. I just need to get somebody to take my place . . . Yo, Rob, take my spot. I'll be back soon."

"Whose team I'm on?" asked Rob

"You on Peanut and Trap Pot's team."

As I ran down the street to my house, holding my shirt against my nose, I left a trail of blood behind me. I hurried up the front steps; my mother and father were sitting on the porch talking with some of their friends.

When she saw me, my mother cried out, "Sugar, what happened?"

"Nothing, ma'am. Dame just stiff-armed the shit out of me and almost broke my damn nose."

"I told you to stay away from them boys," my dad said. "You better stop being so hardheaded." But his words just went in one ear and out the other, as my mother took me inside to clean me up. Once my nose stopped bleeding, she gave me a new shirt and sent me on my way.

I ran straight down Second Avenue to the field and got my spot back from Rob. After playing for a while longer, it started getting dark and most kids had to be home before the streetlights came on. My mother didn't really give us a curfew, so I could stay out as long as I wanted. But I usually went home when the others did.

It was my brother who suggested that my dad sign me up for Pop Warner football down at Bennett Creek in northern Suffolk where all the white kids played. I knew I would never play for the Steelers because I'd overheard my mother telling her friend not to sign her child up for them. My mom didn't like that they'd taken my brother's money but refused to give it back when he couldn't make weight. So my brother somehow convinced my father to sign me up for the Pop Warner team. And my father got my mom to agree to it as well.

The ride to Bennett Creek was long and boring. I was knocked out in the backseat of the van when my brother woke me up.

"We here, Sugar. Get up."

DD Bug knew exactly where to go since he had been to the Creek to watch some of his friends who played in the Pop Warner Midget division. We followed my brother up some steps to a small room, and from there my mother and father did all the talking.

"Excuse me, miss. We are here to sign our daughter up for football."

The lady looked up and said, "You want to sign her up for *football*? Do you mean cheerleading?"

"No," my father replied, "we want to sign her up for football."

The lady just stared at him. "Excuse me, sir, but nobody has never signed their daughter up for football here."

"Well, we want to sign her up for football. Is there a problem?"

"No sir," the lady answered, handing my parents some paperwork.

My father cut the check and my mother filled out the paperwork. While they took care of registering me, my brother and I chatted about what the first practice with Creek would be like. "You ready, Sugar?" DD Bug said.

"Dude, please. I was born ready."

"You better be. You better crack them little dudes up like you be doing back at home."

"You already know, bro."

In some ways, it almost seemed like my brother was more excited than I was.

After that, we all headed out to meet the coach of the Junior Pee Wee team I was going to be on, and to pick up the equipment. From a distance, I could see the team practicing.

My brother was like, "Sugar, there's your coach right there."

I looked at where he was pointing, but all I could

see was some tall, skinny black guy with a small box.

Once we got closer, the lady introduced us: "Meet the Rodgers family. They brought their *daughter* out here to play football."

My brother and I smirked, because my father was a Saunders, not a Rodgers. Our parents weren't even married.

After introducing ourselves to the coach, he introduced me to the team. "Listen up, fellas, we have a new player with us today. Her name is Sugar."

I stood there with my braids hanging straight down my back, wearing a white T-shirt and basketball shorts, looking like a little boy. The kids were shocked and I could hear one of them whisper, "Is that a boy or a girl?"

"Girls don't play football," muttered another kid, while a third one turned to the coach and said, "Are you serious? We have a girl on our team?"

But I didn't pay them any attention as the coach walked me over to collect my equipment. I wasn't used to wearing any of it. In the hood, we just played tackle football without any pads. They fitted me with a helmet, football pants, shoulder pads, and gave me a mouthpiece.

Once I had all my gear, I headed to the bathroom to change—obviously I couldn't change in front of everyone else like the guys did. My mother and brother went with me; outside the bathroom, my brother slipped the pads inside the pants and told me to put them on. I went in, changed, and came out with my white T-shirt tucked into my padded pants, wearing a pair of beat-up tennis shoes. My brother checked my helmet and shoulder pads to make sure I'd put them on correctly, and then I was ready to crack them little dudes up.

My brother walked back with me to the team while my mother joined my father in the stands where most of the parents sat. My brother smacked me on the helmet and told me to put my mouthpiece in. I was more than ready. The coach had told DD Bug that I would need to get some cleats, special football shoes that my father later purchased at the army-navy store.

I remember my first day of practice like it was yesterday. The coach threw me out there on special teams for a kickoff. He could tell I knew a little about football; the game was basically the same as we played in the hood, just a bit more organized. The kicker ran and booted the ball to the other team. I sprinted down the field, breathing hard because I'd never played with a mouthpiece, but somehow managing to keep my eye on the ball. The boy on the other team caught it and before he could get even ten yards, I smacked him so hard it sounded like a gunshot. *Pow!* I had laid the boy out. Matter of fact, I'd hit him so hard he broke his arm from the fall.

I could see my parents looking on, and wasn't really sure how they would react to this, but at the same time I was happy. For the first time in my life, it felt like my brother and I had a special bond that was just our own.

My work ethic was crazy! I was playing golf, basketball, and football at the same time, which kept me away from my friends who I ran the streets with. I would leave school early to go to golf practice and after walking nine or eighteen holes, I would rush home, change clothes, and do my homework before heading over to football practice.

School was very important to my father, and he always made sure I did my homework every afternoon, even before football came into the picture. There were plenty of days when I didn't want to do it, but I had to or I would get a beating. He made sure I got everything correct and everything was neat. If my handwriting was messy, he would make me start over from the beginning.

"But Dad," I would whine, "it's correct. Why I have to start over?"

"It looks sloppy so do it over or you're not going outside."

So I would do it over, but with an attitude. I'd smack my lips, start crying, and would get a beating just that quick.

My siblings were no help and would pick on me while I sat there at the table scowling.

"What you looking at, stupid?" I'd say to my

brother as he walked past, sticking out his tongue or smirking because he'd heard me getting a beating.

"Sugar," my father would say, "just focus and do your work."

"But DD Bug keeps picking on me."

"DeShawn, leave her alone!"

"But Dad, I'm not doing nothing to her," my brother would reply. I'd stick my tongue out at him the second my dad looked away.

I'd definitely have to do it over again after this because there were tears all over the homework, making it look even sloppier.

So, you know, I was heated, but I'd finally get it done, then I'd clean my face up and run outside, happy as could be to finally play with my friends.

CHAPTER 8

TOE-TO-TOE WITH A DRUG DEALER

MOST DAYS AFTER SCHOOL, I went to golf practice. I always went when there was a practice, no matter what. But I remember this one day when I got home from school, and my mom was too sick to take me to practice. Usually, she would have arranged for my dad or a neighbor to drive me if she wasn't able to, but for some reason she hadn't done so.

By this point, I didn't even really want to go to practice. I had continued to lose interest in the sport, and before long I'd come to realize that I really didn't want to play golf at all anymore—but I couldn't tell my mom this or all hell would break loose.

So, I was secretly happy to get the day off, despite the fact that I didn't like to see my mom sick. I changed out of my school clothes and went outside to play basketball with my friends.

It was deep outside that day. Everybody was at the goal by my house. And I mean *everybody*—drug dealers and all. When the dealers were hanging around, they usually took over the goal, and the game quickly became all about money.

Sometimes, we'd play three-on-three and the dealers would take bets on which team would win. Though they were the ones betting money, us kids were playing for bragging rights.

Other times we'd play one-on-one, dollar-a-shot games. I was usually the only young kid playing these games because you had to put up your own money.

When I saw that there was already a dollar-a-shot game in progress, I ran back inside my house yelling, "Mama, can I get some money?"

"For what, Sugar?" she mumbled in her sick voice.

"They playing dollar-a-shot on my goal outside," I said, breathing hard.

"Look in my purse and take five dollars. And don't come in here no more asking me for more money today."

I grabbed five singles out of that purse fast, before she could change her mind. "Thank you, Mama," I said as I took off, running back outside.

Another game had already started, so I had to wait my turn. People who didn't play basketball or weren't that good would stand on the sidelines and place their own bets. I would play in the game *and* place side bets. And I always put my money on me and nobody else.

"I got next!" I yelled, challenging the winner when the game ended. The winner turned out to be one of the neighborhood dealers, a corner boy named Sam who always bet big money.

"You know the rules, Sugar, so let's get started."

The rules were pretty simple: We each got one shot. If you missed, you had to pay the other player a dollar. You played until you ran out of money or until you were finished getting embarrassed in front of everybody.

Sam went first and splashed it. I went next and it rimmed in. He went again and splashed it again. I took my next shot and missed.

"Pay me my money," Sam said with a big smile.

"Pick it up off the ground," I responded with attitude.

In order to play a game, you had to drop your money on the ground. It was a way to verify that you actually had the cash to play. Sometimes, people would try to run off with their money instead of paying up, but you had to be ready to fight if you did that. There were plenty of fights over money.

After Sam picked up my dollar off the ground, I dropped another to keep the game going, leaving me with only three dollars in my pocket.

We kept shooting back and forth, and I ended up winning six games in a row. I was ready to cash out and call it a day, so I turned to Sam and said, "Give me my money."

I could tell he was getting mad that a little girl was beating him. Plus, the guys on the sidelines were talking trash. They always talked trash, whether they were with you or against you.

"One more game, Sugar, but this time let's make it *five* dollars a shot," Sam said.

I paused for a second. I had ten dollars now, and if I lost twice I'd be broke. But then I thought to myself, *Go big or go home, and you already home . . .*

I yelled: "Bet! Put your money where your mouth is!"

He started talking his own trash to the crowd, then pointed to my brother and said, "Bug, I'm about to take your little sister's money."

"She can hold her own," DD Bug said. "I bet fifty dollars on Sugar. Better yet, I got a hundred on my little sister."

Sam shouted, "Bet!" and they both dropped their money.

With more and more bets being placed on the sidelines, I could feel the pressure mounting, some people yelling out words of encouragement, others trying to break my concentration.

"Come on, Sugar, my money on you!"

"Sugar going to lose—she can't handle the pressure!"

"Sugar ain't about that life!"

When all the bets were down, Sam walked past me and said, "Don't crack under the pressure, Sugar."

My stomach dropped.

As the winner of the previous games, I had to shoot first. So I dropped my money and somebody in the crowd passed me the ball. My palms were sweating. I wiped them on my shorts and said to myself, *Sugar, you got this.* I took the first shot and missed it short off the rim. Now it was Sam's turn. He called "Cash!" before he even took the shot, but he hit the rim too, and missed.

"Bet five more dollars, Sugar," he said.

Things were starting to get real. I dropped five more dollars. "I'm all in! That's my last five," I said.

Sam dropped fifty more dollars. "If you beat me, you get all the pot money, plus I'll give you another fifty. Even though I know you not going to beat me."

"Bet!" I countered.

It was his turn to go first. He grabbed the ball and shot; he missed off the left side of the rim. Everyone could see the frustration on his face.

I grabbed the ball out of his hand. "Let me show you how a pro do it."

I shot it in the air while holding my form. I watched it go right through the net—SPLASH!

"Give me my money!" I demanded. I was too hyped to wait, though, and bent down and grabbed the cash, stuffing it in my pocket. I could see everybody who'd bet on me doing the same.

"Run it back," Sam said.

"Naw, not today." I'd gotten my money, so I took off with my friends to the local corner store. They were hyped for me.

"I seen some of y'all cheering for Sam," I said, smiling slyly. We always called each other out.

"I was cheering for you, Sugar," my ride-or-die CJ said immediately.

"I went for the guy because he grown and you a kid," one of my other friends chimed in.

"You better put your money on *me* next time," I said.

They all nodded their heads yes, and I bought all of them something from the store that day.

CHAPTER 9

MY FIRST BASKETBALL TEAM

A COUPLE DAYS LATER, A GUY who went to my mom's church, Mr. Rolling, approached me at my goal and asked if I wanted to be on his basketball team.

"You have to ask my mom," I said.

I wasn't going to ask her if I could play basketball because I already knew the answer. She wasn't going to hesitate—she would say no. She only wanted me to play golf and that's it. She didn't mind me playing any sport around the neighborhood, but if it was up to her, I was going to compete in the LPGA.

I didn't understand why she felt like this. From all the stories I'd heard from the old people in the neighborhood, my mom used to be pretty good at basketball. And anytime somebody saw me shooting hoops and knew I was her daughter, they'd always say, "You play just like your mom."

Mr. Rolling walked up to our house and knocked on the door. Mom opened up and he started talking, trying to convince her, I assumed. I just continued shooting around on my basketball goal—I didn't think he'd have much success changing Mom's mind.

A minute later he said bye to Mom, came back over to the goal, and said, "See you Tuesday!"

I was confused. "See *me* Tuesday?" I mumbled to myself, as Mr. Rolling got in his van and drove off.

I was low-key hyped as I ran into the house.

I played like I didn't know: "Mom, what Mr. Rolling from the church want?"

"Oh, nothing. He just wanted you to play for his basketball team."

"Well, can I?"

"I told him you can, but golf still has to come first."

"Thank you, Mom," I said, then gave her a big hug.

"Golf comes first. Am I clear?"

"Yes, ma'am!"

I ran into my niece's room, smiling from ear to ear.

"Get out, ugly!" she shouted.

I stuck up my middle finger as I backed out of her room.

"You still ugly," she said as she slammed her door.

I went to my brother's room, but he and his friends Scooter and Shawn were playing some video game, and they were so focused on it that I knew there was no point in trying to share my good news. They barely even noticed I was there, so I went to my bedroom and eventually fell asleep.

* * *

A few days went by and before I knew it, it was Tuesday. I couldn't wait to play but I was nervous because I'd never been on an organized basketball team before. I waited on the porch for Mr. Rolling to pick me up.

"You ready to go?" he called out the window of the church van.

"I'm ready. Just let me tell my mom I'm leaving." I opened the screen door and yelled into the house, "My ride here, Mom!"

"Okay, honey. Have fun. I love you!"

"I love you too, Mom, see you later!"

I jumped off the porch and into the van. I was the only person he picked up in my neighborhood. He picked up a couple more girls in a different part of the city before we headed over to the gym where we'd practice.

I had seen some of the girls before, but I wasn't cool with them. They changed into their basketball shoes and started stretching. I just had my Nike Air Force 1 Mid Tops that I always played in. They used to be my school shoes but turned into my play shoes once they got dirty. My mom never allowed me to wear dirty shoes or clothes to school.

I sat on the bench until Mr. Rolling threw me a ball and said I could shoot while the other girls were still stretching. I could tell they were quite familiar with one another; they were all giggling and joking around. I just kept shooting on the basketball goal by myself until Mr. Rolling blew his whistle and all the girls joined him at center court. I stopped shooting and jogged over to the circle they had formed.

"Hi, how's everybody doing today? I'm Mr. Rolling, or Coach Rolling, whichever you prefer to call me. We have a couple new faces here. Please introduce yourselves to the rest of the team."

Everybody looked around, then one girl raised her hand and introduced herself.

I raised my hand next. "My name is Sugar."

All the girls just stared at me.

Mr. Rolling prompted me to continue: "How old are you? What grade are you in? What school do you attend?"

I paused—I hated saying how old I was and what grade I was in, since I was one grade behind. So I just said, "I go to King's Fork Middle School, and I'm in the sixth grade."

Then he asked the returning girls to introduce themselves as well. Most of them were in late middle school and early high school. I was the only sixth grader and apparently the only one who'd never played organized basketball.

"Two-line layups!" Coach Rolling yelled out.

Everybody split up into two lines. I went to the back of one of them, but had no idea what I was supposed to do. I figured I could just follow the leader, and that's what I did.

"Three-man wave!" Coach yelled.

Everybody broke up into three lines, and again, I went to the back of one so I could watch the girls in front of me. I couldn't really figure out what they were doing, and then it was my turn. I was so lost and confused and I kept messing up. I heard one girl whisper, "She must be slow," and nearly all the girls giggled.

I was instantly mad and ready to fight. I hated when people talked about me behind my back. My mom always said, "Sticks and stones may break your bones, but words will never hurt you." And even though words didn't hurt me physically, they made me angry as hell. I knew better, though, than to start a fight at my first practice, so I just told myself, *Sugar, give her buckets whenever you step on the court.*

Finally, another girl, one of the few who hadn't giggled, came over and explained the drill to me.

CHAPTER 10

CITY LEAGUE BASKETBALL

OUR FIRST GAME WAS APPROACHING fast and there weren't many practices left to prepare.

I still didn't know all the rules of the game. I knew the basics and how to put the ball in the basket, but that was about it. Nonetheless, I must have caught on enough as Coach Rolling put me in the starting lineup. A lot of the other girls were upset that they didn't get to start, but I didn't really care—I just wanted to play basketball.

That first game was a disaster. I had never lost so bad in my life. I played pretty well, yet we still lost: by a lot! I mean, we got our butts kicked.

As soon as I got home, I raced into the kitchen to tell my mom about it. I told her how I had played, and she reminded me that basketball was a team sport. She also said she was positive that the next time we played against that same team, we'd win.

Next time came and we lost again . . . and again. We won a couple of our games that year, but the wins were pretty rare. And throughout it all, I kept my promise to my mom and never let basketball interfere with golf.

I was still winning my golf tournaments, but like I said, I just wasn't into the game. So I was really glad she was letting me play basketball, even if the team I was on wasn't all that good.

My mom must have noticed how happy playing basketball made me, since she even let me play in the city league, though not without a little resistance at first.

A lady named Ms. Jennings came up to me after a game with the church team and suggested that I join one of the teams in the city league. She lived across town and her daughter played in the league. I told her it sounded good to me, but that she would have to ask my mom.

"I know her. She's Bob Mae, right? Y'all stay in Williamstown and you have a sister named Sharon?"

I nodded my head yes. A lot of people didn't know I had a sister because she was in prison.

"I'm gonna come to your house and ask your mom if you can play."

"Good luck with that," I said.

"Why you say that?"

"She don't like me playing basketball. I play golf and that comes first. She made that clear when she agreed to let me play for the church team."

"Well, I'm gonna talk to her."

"Okay."

Two days later Ms. Jennings was on my porch

talking to my mom. I couldn't hear what they were saying, but I could see them from my basketball goal. I crossed my fingers.

While our moms were talking, Ms. Jennings's daughter Sheda got out of their green van and came over to play basketball with me. (Sheda was short for Ransheda, but once I got to know her better, I called her by the nickname all her friends used: She-She.) We just chatted it up and shot hoops. She said our moms would probably be talking for a while because her mom could run her mouth. I didn't care—as long as her mom could convince my mom to let me play, it didn't matter to me how long it took.

Before we knew it, the sun was going down and our moms had finally finished up their conversation. Sheda was right: it was a very long talk.

Sheda was really cool and down-to-earth. It turned out we had a lot in common.

After they left, I asked my mom what they were talking about.

She got straight to the point: "You better stop telling people to come around my house asking me can you play basketball. I let you play on Mr. Rolling's team, but that's it."

"I'm good at the game, Mom. That's why they want me to play on their teams."

"I don't care how good you are at basketball. Golf is the only thing you going to play around here from now on."

"But Mom—"

"Don't *But Mom* me. I meant what I said."

I was so mad, I couldn't even look at her, so I went outside and shot on my basketball goal. "I don't know why she won't let me play ball!" I said out loud, as I laid the ball up. "One day she will let me play!"

The next afternoon, Sheda and her mom returned. Ms. Jennings sat on the porch with my mom and they talked. Sheda and I shot hoops and continued getting to know each other.

"What sports do you play?" I asked.

"Basketball and track. What about you?"

"Golf. I really just want to play basketball, but my mom won't let me."

"Why?"

"I'm not sure."

"Well, hopefully she'll let you play on the city team with me," Sheda said.

"I hope so."

When our moms finished talking, Sheda and Ms. Jennings took off in their van. And that's when I learned that somehow, someway, Ms. Jennings had convinced my mom to let me play. But she still reminded me, "Golf comes first."

I didn't care what she said, I just wanted to play basketball. I was nervous about being on a new team with different coaches but I was up for the challenge.

I'd heard that some of the best players in the area were going to be on this team. I was excited to see where I stood, how I stacked up against the others.

On the first day of practice with the city league, Sheda and her mom pulled up outside my house and honked the green van's horn.

"Mama, they here," I called out.

"Okay. See you later, Sugar. I love you."

"I love you too, Mom."

I jumped in the van with a big smile on my face. "Hi, how y'all doing?"

"Good," they both replied.

"I told you I could get you on the team," Ms. Jennings said.

"You did! Thank you so much and thank you for the ride."

"You're welcome. Anytime!"

When we arrived at the elementary school where the team practiced, we put on our shoes and started shooting with the other girls. The coaches were in another room meeting with parents. Once they finished, we huddled up in the middle of the court and we all introduced ourselves, including the coaches.

I knew both of the female coaches from my neighborhood. They told us the team rules and we started practice. It was pretty different than the church team's practices. On this team, we did way more running and had more plays.

We practiced every day that week to get ready for our first game that coming Saturday. We'd be representing Suffolk against a team from Virginia Beach. We'd heard they were pretty good, but our practices had been going very well all week. We didn't care how talented people said they were, we thought we would be better. It was a decent game, and we played well, but we still ended up losing.

I didn't shake nobody's hand after the game, which got me cussed out by the coaches. But I didn't care—I hated losing.

The next day, we had a game against P-town (Portsmouth). We won, though afterward we almost got into a fight with the other team. There was a lot of pushing and shouting back and forth. We didn't care what city you were from: if someone pushed us, we were gonna push back.

CHAPTER 11

THE BUST

WHEN I WAS THIRTEEN YEARS OLD, my mother, who had been diagnosed with lupus years before, became much sicker. It got so bad she could no longer run the candy shop or the household.

It was around this time that my brother hired a crackhead to clean the whole house for a crackhead price. When the guy finished, it looked like a completely different place—it wasn't the house I was used to seeing. The crackhead became our butler of sorts, making sure everything stayed clean both inside and outside the house. While he was a good cleaner, he often made me nervous, because he got high throughout the day.

One time, I was sitting on the porch on a beautiful day, just hanging out with some guys from the neighborhood, when we saw a few cops walking up our street, out of uniform. Anybody could spot a police officer in my neighborhood—pretty much any white guy who looked unfamiliar was police. My front porch was always full of guys hanging out—plucking off the porch, shooting dice, or just chilling. Most of them would take any opportunity to sell crack to get some money.

Now that my mother was so sick, she had no control over the guys on the porch. Whenever my father visited, he was in and out quickly and barely said anything to them. But they weren't *just* neighborhood guys, some were family—my nephews, my brother, and their friends. And I couldn't really complain. DD Bug was trying to get that money to provide for the whole family, something my mother could no longer do.

We relied on food stamps my whole life, even though my mother worked two jobs until she got too sick. She did receive child support, but it was never quite enough. And now my mother, our backbone, was ill and we had nobody else to turn to.

So my siblings and I turned to the streets to get that fast money. And, of course, it wasn't just money for food and other essentials; DD Bug made sure I had the hottest shoes, and my niece Kakie made sure I had the finest clothes, procured with her five-finger discount. I also kept a little pocket money from the child support checks. After forging my mother's signature, I'd pay the bills while squirreling away some for myself. My nephews also chipped in with a few dollars here and there whenever they could. So we worked together to make sure we had a roof over our heads, food on the table, and clothes on our backs. My siblings, niece, and nephews always made sure I was taken care of because I was the youngest of them all.

But back to that day when I was sitting there on the porch, minding my own business. The plain-clothes policemen looked like they were going to walk right past our house, when a cop car screeched up. Several uniformed officers jumped out and ran straight towards us.

"Get down on the ground!" they shouted. "Everybody is under arrest!"

While I'd seen stuff like this on the block before, it had never happened to me. Before I could even think straight, the cops ran right into the house and started ordering everyone who was inside to come out.

After the officers got almost everybody out of the house and on the ground, they started questioning people, asking how old they were. But no one would answer.

Eventually they got to me. I told them my name was Ta'Shauna Rodgers and that I was only thirteen, so they didn't put me in handcuffs.

One cop barked at me, "Sit in this chair and don't move. We will have somebody call your parents."

"My mother's in the house. So can I move now?"

"No. Stay right there until we tell you to move."

The police were always causing so many problems in the hood, and by now I pretty much hated them. But I kept quiet and stayed seated. From the chair, I looked around and saw about five guys in handcuffs, including my oldest nephew, Vanshawn. The police lined them up outside on the porch then continued to search the house.

When most of the cops were inside, Vanshawn whispered to me, "Sugar, grab everything out my pocket."

I was nervous since I had no idea what he had in there, but I quickly stuck my hand in and grabbed everything.

"Keep my phone and my money," he said.

"Where the rest of it at?" My nephew sold drugs so I just knew he had a pack on him.

"I don't have nothing on me. I'm gonna call the phone, so make sure you pick up."

"I'm gonna give it to Kakie," I said, as Vanshawn was escorted to the police car that would take him downtown to the police headquarters.

When something goes down on the block, the whole neighborhood rushes to the scene, and that day, the scene was our house. There were so many people watching what was happening, while I just sat there looking around at everyone. I could hear people whispering, "What happened? What happened?" And I was thinking, *Shut the fuck up. You're just a bunch of nosy-ass neighbors.*

As I'd told the cops, my mother was in the house, but they didn't make her come out. She was so sick at this point that she couldn't walk or even really talk.

In fact, taking care of my mother had become a nine-to-five job for me. I hardly went to school, because I was my mother's nurse. I had to lift her from the bed to the chair and then back again just to make sure she was clean. I washed her often, and every time I would get an upset stomach from the sight of her dirty diaper. The smell of waste and urine left me literally gagging. Despite this, I found something deep inside of myself to not give up on her.

Trust me, she was about 130 pounds of dead weight. And while I didn't give up, there were definitely some days that I was too tired to even lift her; sometimes she would end up lying in bed with a disgusting diaper for a couple hours or so until I could find the energy to wash her.

To make matters worse, our washing machine and dryer didn't work, so I'd have to hand-wash everything and then find somewhere to hang it up to dry in the house. Sometimes, I'd opt to bring it to the nearby laundromat.

When she could manage to eat, I would make her chicken noodle soup or my father would take me to get her favorite—a fish combo from McDonald's.

Eventually, my brother hired a girl in the hood who was a certified nurse to come over and take care of her, so that Kakie and I could get a break. We didn't have health insurance so my brother paid the nurse in cash.

Although my mother was too sick for the police to make her leave the house, they did call an ambulance. They said they couldn't just leave her to live in these conditions. I was sitting there thinking to myself, *What conditions are they talking about?* They said nobody could stay in our house, because it was not in livable shape.

Before my mother had gotten sick, she'd always said she wanted to die at home, so I knew she wouldn't want to leave the house, no matter what condition it was in.

She looked like she was on death's door when the medics came in the ambulance to take her away. After they left with her and the cops took everyone down to the station who they'd found drugs on, the city sent a man right away to inspect the house.

The inspector quickly decided that it was not up to the city's building codes, and he placed a big, fat orange *Condemned* sticker on the window. My family home was taken by the City of Suffolk because of a drug bust.

They told us to get whatever we needed for the night, and then said that after that no one could go back in the house. As soon as Kakie found out about the bust, she left work and came right home, arriving just after everything was over.

I told Kakie what had happened, and the police also filled her in, but she wasn't trying to hear any of that shit. She went off and started talking crazy to the police while I tried to keep her calm. Kakie is like that. She goes from 0 to a 100 real quick. She was devastated that we had nowhere to go, nobody to turn to. We were now officially homeless. Tears started rolling down our faces as we accepted this new reality.

The police guarded the house that night to make sure we didn't go back in. But the next day when the cops were gone, the rest of the family and I went back in to take some of our things out before they returned. We knew that if we got caught, we'd be in big-time trouble, but like we always said, *Fuck the police*. We needed our stuff.

As days went by, we had to find places to sleep every night. Sharon's kids went to stay with their father, and DD Bug stayed with his girlfriend.

The one person I had initially thought would take me in was my father. Nope, not in this lifetime. Instead I was taken in by one of my basketball coaches, who let me stay with her and her family, but it was nothing like home.

I never asked my father why he didn't take me in, but I'm assuming his wife was a big part of it. My dad had six children—a daughter by his first wife, three children with his second wife . . . and, oh, don't forget the two out of wedlock: my brother and me. My father lived a double life. He had both a wife and a baby mother—*my* mother.

* * *

Those first few days after we'd been kicked out, we continued to try to rescue more of our belongings from our condemned house, but little did we know that the following week the whole thing would be gone. They tore it down with our belongings in it.

While the city called our house unlivable, to us it was the best home we could ever have asked for. And just like that, all of our family memories were gone—the golf trophies I'd won, our clothes, everything gone just like that.

Although it seemed like we'd hit rock bottom, things only continued to go downhill from there.

A couple weeks later, I had to tell my mother that her sister Amanda had died in Maryland, but at this point she was so sick she didn't understand anything I said to her over the phone. It was Kakie who made sure I visited my mother every so often at the nursing home. She'd pull up outside my coach's home beeping her car horn and shouting, "Sugar, come on! Dang, I'm outside!" I'd respond that I could hear the horn, that there was no need to be shouting too, but she'd just say, "Y'all should've been ready when I got here. Dang!"

So the day before I was set to go on a long trip to Florida with my AAU (Amateur Athletic Union) team, Kakie drove me to the nursing home to visit with my mom before leaving.

She arrived in her usual fashion, laying on her

horn as she pulled up out front. Mind you, she was also calling me on my phone at the same time.

"Sugar, come on! Dang, I'm outside!"

"I'm coming. I can hear you blowing."

"Y'all should have been ready when I got here. Dang!" she yelled as She-She and I jumped into the backseat.

Kakie spent the entire drive on her phone, cussing out one friend, talking to other homegirls about something else. I didn't pay her much attention, but I did hear her tell someone, "Girrrrl, we headed to see my grandmother at the nursing home. My aunt Sugar's leaving for Florida tomorrow so I'm just taking her before she go on her trip."

The drive should have been about fifteen minutes, but the way my niece drove it took about nine. She blasted the music and She-She and I sat in the backseat laughing and joking around.

Once we arrived at the nursing home, though, the laughing and joking stopped. I didn't like going there. The atmosphere was depressing—people who were really sick or just so old that they couldn't do much for themselves anymore. I'll never forget the smell either. As soon as the nurse buzzed me into the facility, the odor overwhelmed me—it smelled like very old people.

When I shared the terrible news about Aunt Amanda with my mother, she just looked at me and smiled, like everything was going to be okay.

CHAPTER 12

THE TOURNAMENT

A DATE I WILL NEVER FORGET: JULY 12, 2005. My basketball team, the Suffolk Blazers, took the longest
van ride imaginable, driving from Suffolk to Orlando,
Florida, only stopping twice for food and twice to
use the restroom. It was the first trip I'd ever taken
without my mother, and when I'd visited her in the
nursing home the night before we left, I told her
how much I loved her and how well taken care of
I'd be with my coaches. I was anxious, but also
excited.

We were on our way to an AAU basketball tournament. In the van, my teammates and I talked about
everything; we shared secrets, cracked jokes, and
sang along to different songs on the radio. We passed
the time playing games like truth or dare, spades, and
punch buggy. Punch buggy was my favorite—you had
to look out the window, try to find a VW Beetle, and
if you were the first one to spot it, you got to punch
everybody on the arm.

Florida was amazing—I had never seen tropical
hardwood hammock trees before. The surroundings

were just incredible. I can remember looking out the window and pointing at everything that caught my eye.

Arriving at the hotel was the best feeling in the world after being cramped up in the van for twelve hours. I could finally stretch out and relax before the tournament began. Because my mother was too sick to come, I roomed with Ransheda and her mother, Ms. Jennings, who treated me as if I were her daughter. In addition to convincing my mom to let me play AAU basketball, Ms. Jennings had also helped me fundraise so I could make it onto the team.

After we checked into the hotel, we had time to do some exploring and gift shopping for friends and family back home. Later, when we returned to the hotel, I started feeling down. She-She told me I was probably just homesick and would be fine in the morning, but I wasn't so sure. Something about being there didn't feel right.

We took showers and changed into our pajamas. Instead of going to bed, however, we met up with some of our other teammates in the hallway and went down to the hotel lobby. We ended up meeting some boys who were there for a track meet, and hung out with them talking and joking. Eventually we decided it would be fun to play chase throughout the hotel. First, we would chase the boys, then they would chase us. During the game, She-She and I thought it would be a good idea to go hide in our room. We ran back there, slamming the door behind us and giggling. But right then Ms. Jennings said in a sleepy voice, "Don't y'all go back outta this room."

We were disappointed we couldn't return to the game, but we lay there quietly until we finally fell asleep.

The next morning we had a meeting downstairs before we headed out to the game. Some of my teammates were in trouble because they'd gotten caught the night before in the boys' hotel rooms. The parents of one of our teammates were so strict, we knew she'd be in a heap of trouble if they found out she'd been in a boy's hotel room too, so we lied and said she'd been with us.

After the team meeting, we headed out to our first game of the tournament . . . and we won! Before we celebrated at dinner, I called Kakie to tell her about our victory and to check on how everyone was doing. When I asked how my mother was, Kakie responded, "Everything is okay." So I hung up, and joined the rest of my team inside the restaurant to eat and talk about the game.

The following morning, July 14, 2005, we got up and headed downstairs for a big breakfast before our next game. As I was eating with my teammates, one of my coaches said, "Sugar, I need to talk to you about something. Come upstairs to my room once you finish." I thought it was something related to the game, so as soon as I was done eating, I headed upstairs to her room.

I sat down on the small couch in her suite and she sat next to me and said, "I love you and if you ever need anything, I'm here for you."

I wasn't quite sure why she was telling me this now, but I said I'd let her know if I needed anything and that I loved her too.

"I didn't bring you up here just to tell you that. Sugar, your mother passed away this morning. I am so sorry about this."

I was at a loss for words and started crying immediately, while millions of thoughts rushed through my head. *Who's going to take care of me? Will I go into foster care? Will my dad be willing to take me in now?*

I was devastated and shocked. Of course I knew how sick she was, but I'd always assumed I would be there to say my last goodbyes. When I went back downstairs, everyone kept saying, "Sorry to hear about your mother," and I immediately broke down and started crying again. My coach held me in her arms like my mother would have done.

After I got myself together, I headed out to our next game with my team. I knew everyone must have been thinking, *Why is Sugar playing? Her mother just died, she needs to be taking it easy.* But I knew that if my mother had been there she would have wanted me to do the right thing. And for me, the right thing was playing. I knew she was looking down on me as I played in that game. I ended up scoring several times and we won. In a way, the game was a good distraction for me at that moment. I was able to stop thinking about my mother and just focus on getting buckets. It was my way of coping and getting my mind off the whole situation for a little while.

But I couldn't ignore reality for too long. That night I told my team that I was going back home to be with my family because they needed me. My teammates understood, and wished me a safe trip back while they stayed and played in the rest of the tournament. One of our coaches drove me, and the twelve-hour ride seemed even longer than it had going down since all I did was think about my mother's death. So many things were running through my head: *How is my family holding up? Why did God choose her now? Will I be able to go on without her?*

CHAPTER 13

THE FUNERAL

WHEN I GOT HOME FROM FLORIDA, I just wanted to be alone. I didn't want to be around friends or family. I lay in bed for days, contemplating my future. I couldn't even picture a life without my mother. My family encouraged me to go view her body but I never did because I just couldn't handle it. I never got the chance to express these feelings, though, because I needed to be strong for my family.

Instead of viewing the body, I went shopping for something to wear to the funeral. I picked out a nice white blouse with a black skirt and some baby doll shoes. I hated wearing skirts, but it was important to my mother, so I did it for her. I knew it would make her proud that I'd worn a skirt to her funeral, that nobody had to force me.

July 19 at 11 a.m. was the homegoing service for my mother, Barbara Mae Rodgers, at the Bethlehem Christian Church in Williamstown. People from all over the city joined family and friends from out of town to see my mother for the last time. I got ready at my coach's house and then she dropped me off at my aunt and uncle's place.

My brother, niece, nephew, uncle, and I all rode in the limo that the funeral home provided, while my father followed in his own car. Sharon couldn't be there because she was in prison at the time and the facility had denied her request. We'd spoken on the phone, and I could hear in Sharon's voice just how upset she was—not just to be missing the funeral, but also because she couldn't be there with us when we needed her most. In addition to all that, Sharon's son, my nephew Vanshawn, was also in jail now. He'd gotten locked up the day before my mother died on a false murder charge.

On the ride over, everybody was in pretty good spirits, laughing and joking around. The air conditioner didn't work in the limo so we were all sweating by the time we got to the church. Once we arrived, though, we started to quiet down. The place was so packed we couldn't park in front like one normally would; we had to park about a block away.

I got out of the vehicle and immediately went to look for Kakie's son, Mo, who was three at the time, and my brother's son, Keagan, who was two; I found that spending time with Mo and Keagan helped, as I was able to focus on their childish antics and distract myself from my sadness.

A bunch of people from the hood were decked out in hastily made *RIP Mother of the Town* T-shirts, while others wore shirts that said *Free* with a long list of everyone from the town who was currently in jail.

The baby-blue casket my mother was lying in was closed, with a bouquet of flowers on top. As soon as the preacher started talking, my family and I were immediately in tears, listening to all the great things he had to say about my mother and how important she was to the whole community. He would get off topic sometimes, talking about the guys who stood on the corner selling drugs, which had nothing to do with my mother's funeral, but I guess it was okay.

After the sermon, the choir sang, and then there was an open mic where people could get up and share their memories of my mother. You could hear people crying, sniffling, and chatting the whole time.

At some point, this one lady started singing opera, which sent Kakie and me into a fit of giggles. While we didn't know this for sure, we imagined that my mother wouldn't be too interested in having an opera-singing lady at her funeral. For some reason this just made us laugh even more.

After all the singing and talking, it was time for everyone to say their goodbyes. At some point during the service, someone from the church had opened the casket lid, and now people from the back rows started lining up to pay their respects. When it came time for our row to go up, Kakie went first. She approached the casket and gently touched my mother's face before bending over and giving her a kiss. She stayed leaning over the coffin and hugged my mother so hard that she nearly pulled her body out of the coffin. Kakie was so upset that she had to be helped out of the church.

And then it was my turn. I could see my mother lying in that casket looking as beautiful as ever. I knew this would be my last time resting my eyes on her. Still seated, I looked at my brother, nephew, and father, all with tears streaming down their faces. I just sat there taking it all in. It was the worst feeling of my life.

I was weeping as I stepped forward and leaned in to kiss my mother. She was so cold and stiff and the kiss was unlike the warm and tender ones she used to give me. My only comfort was knowing she was now in a better place—a place where there would be no suffering, no struggle, and no worries. I hoped that by focusing on this, I'd find the strength to continue on with my own life, but we were all so devastated—the heart and soul of our family had died and gone to heaven.

CHAPTER 14

DD BUG

AFTER LOSING BOTH MY FAMILY HOME and my mother, I thought things couldn't get any worse. But right away, I noticed that DD Bug had started acting different, strange even. I didn't know if it had anything to do with the friends he was hanging out with, but he'd say some fool things like, "Sugar, I'm God, I'm untouchable and unstoppable." And I'm thinking to myself, *What is wrong with him?*

One time we were in his car and he said, "Sugar, look at that building. The feds are watching me, but they can't catch me." I couldn't even figure out what building he was talking about.

I called my dad and told him DD Bug was acting strange. It turns out my dad knew what was wrong, but he didn't tell me at the time. In fact, the whole city was talking about DD Bug. One Saturday, I got a call that my brother was running down the street butt naked squawking like a chicken.

Finally, two of my cousins, along with Ransheda's mother, tricked him into going to the hospital by telling him it was a car dealership and that they were taking him to buy a new vehicle. We felt we had to lie to get him the help he clearly needed.

While I waited in the car, the others went into the hospital to check my brother in. At first, DD Bug sat quietly, sweating in the heavy winter coat he wore, despite the summer heat. I watched through the car window as some police arrived at the hospital. When DD Bug noticed the cops heading towards him, he stood up as if he was going to go with them peacefully. But I knew how much my brother hated the cops. Sure enough, he started fighting with them as soon as they reached him, throwing things around and at the cops. I had never seen my brother act so crazy. It took at least fifteen police to get him under control, and when they finally did, they took him away in handcuffs. He ended up going to jail because there were outstanding warrants for his arrest.

I would later find out that one of his so-called friends had given him some "Love Boat"; it was this PCP-based drug that had caused all of his bizarre behavior. It was awful to see what drugs could do to a person, but I was glad he was finally getting help.

CHAPTER 15

LIFE AT COACH BETTY'S HOUSE

EVEN BEFORE OUR HOUSE WAS CONDEMNED and my mother died, I spent a good amount of time at my coach's house. But after I lost both my family home and mother, I'd moved in more permanently. Even though she had two young sons, Coach Betty took me in with open arms. I was very lucky, because she made time for me and all my extracurricular activities. During my time there, her two children, her sister, and her sister's kids lived there as well. It was a three-bedroom apartment, and I would usually sleep on the couch.

One night after trying to get comfortable on the couch, and failing, I moved into the kids' room and slipped into the bottom bunk with my coach's youngest son, who was six or seven at the time. After a good night's sleep, though, I woke up freezing cold and covered in piss. I knew he still peed the bed, but damn, did he have to piss all over me?

Mostly, it was fun being there, but sometimes, I felt left out because it wasn't my real family. Coach Betty continued to work hard, and eventually we were able to move into our own apartment with two bedrooms—one for Coach and a second one that I shared with her two sons. I was amazed that she could balance the amount of work she did with being a single parent taking care of two sons and a teenage girl who wasn't even her family.

For a couple months, life seemed good, but then Coach started dating this new guy. Things started to change as soon as he came into the picture. We stopped having "family time," and Coach seemed to have less and less time to spend with me and even her own sons.

Some days I would arrive home to find her crying, asking her older son Dre for advice on which man she should be with. "Should I choose my ex-husband or my new boyfriend?" she would ask him. Dre always told his mother she should choose her ex-husband. When I asked him why he thought that, he simply said he didn't believe the new boyfriend was right for her.

Despite Dre's advice, a few weeks after this exchange, we moved again—into a house with her boyfriend in Portsmouth. My whole world was changing. I was a teenager dealing with a lot of stress—the pressure of having to move to Portsmouth, possibly change schools, and be farther away from what I had left of a family.

So I made a couple of calls, because I wanted to continue to play basketball at King's Fork High

School. Luckily, the school also wanted me to keep playing there, so every morning one of the teachers would come pick me up in Portsmouth and drive me to King's Fork. I also had my father write a letter to the school board asking if I could continue attending King's Fork and guaranteeing that I would have a ride to school every day.

While I didn't want to live in Portsmouth, the move there meant I'd have my own bedroom for the first time in my life. I didn't like the view from my window, though: a church and a graveyard. This seemed like a bad omen to me.

One crazy thing about my living situation was that even though I was paying my coach rent at this point, I was never given my own damn house key. My dad gave me $250 around the first of every month for living expenses. Somehow my dad was receiving his own child support, but that's a whole other story. Out of that $250, I would keep $150 for myself and give the rest to Coach Betty. I also got a small additional allowance from my dad, and I had some of my own money from selling candy to other kids before and after school.

I just didn't understand why I couldn't have my own key when I was paying rent. There were plenty of times when I would get dropped off after school and have to wait outside for hours before Coach got home. I'd ask for a key, but she would always put it off, saying, "I'll get you one soon." After months of waiting, I finally realized I wasn't getting one. And it wasn't because she was forgetting—it was because of her new lover.

One thing I knew was that anyone who had children understood that kids are going to be kids. They are not always going to make their beds, take out the trash, or wash the dishes on their own—that's why they need parents to instill responsibility in them. So it wasn't that I resented helping out around the house . . . but every day we were given a list of chores, and it seemed as if every day it was the same list. Sometimes I found myself thinking, *How can I clean something that's already clean?*

Life in the house got more and more outrageous. Sometimes Coach and her boyfriend wouldn't allow us to eat the household food. I felt that if my father was paying for me to live there, I should be able to eat some of the food. Well, I guess not.

It got to the point where I finally asked Kakie if I could use her food-stamp card to get snacks and extra food for me and the two boys. As soon as Kakie found out about my situation, she made sure to bring us snacks every month. But our food was still kept separate from theirs. How can you separate your food from your own children? I kind of understood not sharing with me (even though it seemed totally unfair), but keeping food from her boys? I couldn't understand that at all.

I remember one time there was a box of a hundred packs of animal crackers in the kitchen cabinet. But they'd rather let those crackers go stale than share them with us. I felt especially sorry for Dre because his father was not in his life, so he had no one else he could even consider staying with. I could at least go crash with family every so often, or I would stay with my cousin Keda, who also happened to be the assistant coach of the Suffolk Blazers. I loved going to Keda's. We'd play basketball and jump on the trampoline—all the kids loved her house. I wished I could stay there forever. I had never asked Keda if I could stay with her before because I was scared she would say no. Regardless, her house was always open to me. Getting out of Coach Betty's house, even just for a short while, was like a Monopoly *Get Out of Jail Free* card—a pass that I would take any day!

One afternoon, I invited a guy from school over. Coach Betty and her boyfriend weren't home, but her two boys were in the house, so I didn't let the guy inside. Instead we sat in his car talking. When Coach and her boo pulled up, she didn't even notice us sitting there, and when she entered the house she asked her sons where I was.

"You didn't see Sugar outside in the car?" Dre said.

As soon as I walked in, Coach and I got into a huge argument. She asked me who I was talking to in the car, and I was like, "Just a guy."

"Who is this guy?" she demanded, and when I replied that he was a friend from school, she snapped, "Give me your phone!"

I refused, so she tried to punish me. And trust me, punishment around that house was no joke. It seemed the longer I stayed there, the worse things got. They made me pay for a cable box, and then took it away as punishment. Because Coach didn't want anyone else at school to know where she lived, I often wasn't allowed to be dropped off in front of the house. Sometimes this meant I'd end up walking late at night, by myself.

I couldn't take it anymore. I had to move out. I didn't care where I went, and after our big argument, I knew I couldn't stay in that house one more day. I felt guilty about leaving the two boys behind, but I didn't know what else to do.

So I packed my clothes and called Kakie to come pick me up. She asked where I was going, and I explained that I didn't know, but I couldn't live with Coach Betty and her boyfriend any longer. I was so miserable there that I couldn't even look Coach in the eye anymore. She was blinded by love and so afraid of being alone that she was letting this man make all the household decisions, and the way he ran things just wasn't something I could deal with.

I'll never forget the expression on Dre's face when I was leaving. It reminded me of the look on a child's face that you see on one of those TV commercials about kids starving in third world countries. He wanted the love and attention from his mother that he used to get. The thing that I could never understand was that her boyfriend was a *teacher*! I mean, how can you take care of the kids at your school, but then turn around and totally neglect the children in your own house? How could you deny them the love, affection, and attention that all kids need?

In my mind, you can't love a man who doesn't treat your kids well. It's a package deal. I don't have kids and even *I* know that.

And even though, as I packed my bags to leave, I had a lot of anger towards Coach Betty, I was determined not to carry that negativity with me. I told myself that the way she had treated me would only make me stronger. Though I certainly don't want to give her any credit she might run with. Just saying.

I did appreciate her taking me in when I didn't have anywhere else to go. She also showed me how blind love can be. Yet probably the most important thing I learned from living there was how *not* to raise my future children. And I will never choose a man over my offspring. Love will never be that blind for me. Those are the important lessons I took with me when I moved out of Coach Betty's house.

CHAPTER 16

AUNT LINDA

WHEN I LEFT COACH BETTY'S PLACE, I went to live with Aunt Linda, back in Suffolk. Linda had married my mother's younger brother, Uncle Junie, who'd died two years after my mother. Aunt Linda's four children were all grown up and out of the house, so she lived alone.

When I'd called to ask if I could come stay with her, she didn't hesitate for a second before saying yes. She asked what was wrong, of course.

"I can't stay here anymore!" I said through my tears. "This bitch is driving me crazy!"

"Calm down," my aunt replied, "I'm here. Come over to my house."

So Kakie picked me up and we headed straight to Aunt Linda's.

Kakie had always been my ride-or-die. She saw a lot in me that I couldn't see in myself. In fact, she had wanted to take me in after we'd lost the family home, but she didn't have her own place. She went to stay with DD Bug and his girlfriend at the time, and it wasn't her responsibility to find me a place to live too. Besides, she thought Coach Betty's might be a better place for me.

We drove to Aunt Linda's listening to music on the radio, while I stared out the window with tears rolling down my face. Kakie was practically in tears herself.

Once we arrived, I cleaned up my face in the car. I knew my aunt had wanted to take me in long before, but I'd always found other places to stay because I didn't want to trouble her and my uncle. Especially since they had always been very supportive of my mother and the rest of us. But now it was different, and I truly felt like I had nowhere else to go.

Kakie and I unloaded the car while Aunt Linda made up a bed for me. After unpacking, Kakie ran me over to the nearby Walmart to pick up a few things. While we were there, I tried calling my aunt to see if there was anything she needed, but I kept getting a recording saying, *"Your phone has been temporarily disconnected."*

I was like, *I know my phone can't be off, I just paid the phone bill!* But then I paused for a moment. I had bought the phone in my coach's name, because at the time I hadn't been old enough to get one in my own name.

I turned to my niece. "This stupid bihhh turned my phone off."

"She dirty for that," Kakie replied as she walked towards the cashier.

On the ride back to my aunt's house, I called my father to ask him to get me a phone in his name.

The next morning, I woke up early to a delicious smell. When I went into the kitchen, I discovered that my aunt had cooked us a huge breakfast: sausage, bacon, eggs, French toast, and iced tea.

"Go brush your teeth and wash your face, and then come eat," Aunt Linda said. That morning was the fastest I'd ever gone in and out the bathroom. When I came back into the kitchen, my aunt handed me a plate of food.

"If you want more, just help yourself. Make yourself at home."

I ate that food in no time and went for seconds before my father arrived to take me to the Sprint store so he could add me to his phone plan. I was in my room getting ready when I heard, *Beep! Beep! Ring! Beeeep! Ring! Ring*! My father was simultaneously calling the house and blowing his horn for me to come out. I raced outside.

The ride to the Sprint store was relatively quiet, until my dad said, "Your coach called and told me what happened."

"What she say?"

"Just that you moved out, and something about you having a guy over."

"Oh yeah, I did have a guy over, but he never came inside the house. He's a friend from school and we just talked for a few minutes in his car. Then she tried to take my phone away as punishment. For what, I don't know and I don't care. I pay my own phone bill and you can't just take something that don't belong to you."

My father didn't say anything more, but I could tell he felt guilty then about not taking me in. He couldn't really reprimand me because, in a way, it was his own fault that I was going through this foolishness.

At the Sprint store, I got a red Razr with unlimited minutes. My dad added me to his family plan, and I was so glad I wouldn't have to worry anymore about coming up with money to pay my bill every month. I stored all my numbers in my new phone, bought a ringtone, and immediately called Kakie and She-She to give them my new number.

At Aunt Linda's house, there weren't many rules or chores I had to do. All she really wanted from me was to do well in school and stay out of trouble. My aunt knew I wasn't a troublemaker. She knew I kept myself occupied playing sports and hanging with She-She.

Every weekday morning, my aunt would knock on my bedroom door. I would call through the closed door, "I'm up," and she would go back to bed. Sometimes I would get up, but most of the time I wouldn't. Whenever we had a basketball game, though, I went to school, even if I only went for half a day or spent most of my time in the nurse's office.

Despite my inconsistent attendance, I had okay grades—mostly Cs. I really didn't like school, but I loved playing basketball, and the two went hand in hand. Out of 180 days of school, I probably made it there about half the time. I would forge my own absence notes, sometimes signing my mother's name, sometimes my aunt's. My mother had been dead for a few years at that point, so you know the school wasn't paying attention like they should've been. They just wanted some type of note excusing the absence.

Most teachers knew I was a good kid, but they also knew I was going through a lot. And while I was relatively well-behaved, I couldn't stand to have any teachers disrespecting me.

Some of the teachers seemed like they wanted to be there as little as I did. But one of the assistant principals, Mr. Q, was one of the coolest adults I knew. Without him I don't know how I would have made it through school. He gave me so many chances. I was open with him, so he knew what I was dealing with and what I had been through.

I had been written up so many times over the years that my school records folder looked nearly as thick as one of my science books. People would say Mr. Q was giving me extra chances because I played basketball—but that wasn't true. He genuinely wanted me to accomplish something in life.

I probably would have dropped out in tenth grade if it wasn't for basketball and Mr. Q. The game was truly a lifesaver for me.

CHAPTER 17

BOO WILLIAMS

SINCE STARTING HIGH SCHOOL, I'd spent my summers playing basketball for the Suffolk Blazers. I liked my team and didn't have any plans to go elsewhere, but one day I received an invitation to try out for Boo Williams's AAU basketball team. And as I mentioned, I hadn't planned to leave the Blazers, but at the same time, I couldn't ignore such an opportunity.

The day of the tryouts, I was nervous—I didn't know anybody. The other girls trying out were from all over the 757. The AAU tryouts brought together the top girls from seven eastern Virginia cities along with some girl from a town way up north in the state. Most of the girls had already made the team the year before, so the pressure was on! I had to represent for my city.

The first day went smoothly. I made the first cut and was onto the second day. I felt uneasy about the other girls, especially the ones who'd made the team the year before and seemed to have so much confidence. I had never taken basketball as seriously as they did. It was something I did to stay out of trouble; playing basketball took my mind off all the things that I had going on in my life.

But this tryout was more intense and real than I had anticipated. We did a couple of drills, played five-on-five. Drills were certainly not my thing. I was that unorthodox player who couldn't pull off things in practice, but somehow ended up doing them in the game. I loved playing five-on-five—that was easy to me. I did that at the gym when I skipped school or with my friends in the hood.

So when we played five-on-five during tryouts, and I got buckets, I thought to myself, *There is no way Boo is going to cut me now.* And I was right: later that day I received a call saying I had made the team. I remained calm on the phone, but in my mind I was jumping up and down with excitement. And while I rarely expressed my emotions out loud, I did call Kakie. I always shared my good news with her and she was always happy for me.

Once I was officially on Boo Williams's AAU team, we got the game schedule along with some new gear. I wasn't used to getting new gear without having to stand outside Walmart raising money by selling candy bars or hosting car washes. We had to fundraise a lot for the Suffolk Blazers because the team didn't have any money.

But when Boo handed out all that new Nike gear— socks, flip-flops, shoes, gym bag, and T-shirts—I couldn't believe what I was seeing. Having that Nike check on all my gear made me feel like an elite player. Also, I was happy I didn't have to fundraise in the hot sun. Don't get me wrong, fundraising was fun sometimes—but most of the time it was a pain in the ass.

Our first tournament was the Boo Williams Nike Invitational in Hampton, Virginia. It was a must that we win our own tournament. Although I was accustomed to starting, I wasn't starting in this first game. A girl who'd been on the team the previous year was starting, which made sense to me—Boo knew her strengths and weaknesses, while he was still learning mine.

I took a seat on the bench and watched. But soon, I noticed how quickly the time was rolling off the clock, and I still wasn't getting called in to sub for anybody. Finally, Boo called my name. I was subbing for a girl whose name I couldn't even remember.

I was excited and also nervous when the ball came towards me the first time in that game. I dove for it and ended up getting fouled for two free throws. I went up to the line—missed the first, but made the second. Mind you, I had just come off the bench, but most of the other girls had been playing the whole game and were definitely showing signs of fatigue. I was cool as ice, with plenty of energy.

I ended up playing for about five minutes. And we won!

After shaking hands with our opponents, we headed back into the locker room to have a team meeting. Boo talked a little about the game, but I wasn't trying to hear it, I was ready to get out of there.

I had never scored only one point in my career. Once I got to the car, I sat in the backseat where nobody could see me and quietly cried; I was both overwhelmed and frustrated.

A couple games passed and I wasn't called up to play at all. At this point, I really wanted to quit, yet I didn't. I stayed on the team. Soon we'd made it to the championship game, but I wasn't that excited since I figured I wouldn't end up playing.

From my seat on the bench, I had a great view of everything and I could spot several college coaches in the audience. I knew nothing about college, though I'd been told that I could likely get a basketball scholarship. I didn't know if this was true or bullshit—people will tell you anything to get you on their team in the 757. I wasn't planning on going to college after high school anyway. I was going to head straight into the army with She-She.

By the third quarter of the championship game, we were down by twenty points. When Boo called me in to sub, I was thinking, *Don't put me in the game when we already losing by twenty*. But I knew I had to play my best, so I just put my head down and didn't even look up at the scoreboard for a while.

When I did finally look up, we had cut the other team's lead down to ten. I was getting plenty of buckets . . . until I twisted my ankle. And even though we didn't win, I finished the game with thirteen points.

Boo and his staff must have seen something promising in me, because once my ankle healed I got a lot of playing time and I was getting bucket after bucket. I was excited to now be the sixth girl off the bench.

The next tournament was at the Milk House in Florida; it was a tournament that I'd played in before with the Suffolk Blazers. That drive from Virginia was stupid long, and it was hard to get comfortable in the van. I always shared a seat with Boo's nephew—he would lie on the floor in the back and I would stretch out across the seat.

Once we arrived, I learned that instead of sleeping in a hotel as I'd assumed, we were actually staying in a few six-bedroom houses. Once the staff assigned us to a house, everybody took off running through it like you see them girls doing on that Flavor Flav TV show. I waited for everyone in my assigned house to run off and then I walked upstairs to a room with twin beds that nobody seemed to want. I didn't care which room I slept in—I just wanted my own space for a change.

I got comfortable—unpacked my things and took a shower. I didn't really like Florida because it reminded me of the last time I'd been there; I would always associate that state with my mom's death. So I wasn't really feeling it, and therefore, I didn't want to go out and explore the area. I just wanted to stay in the house, silently hoping that one of my teammates would bring me back something to eat. None of them knew me very well, because I was never very open with them. I did talk to Boo's mother when we went on road trips, and she was hilarious. But mostly I kept to myself.

The next morning I woke up early to get ready for the game. We had to be in the van at a certain time or it would leave without us. I made sure I was there a little too early just in case I forgot something and had to run back to the house to get it.

In the huddle just before the game, Boo said, "Sugar, you will start." I was jittery because I couldn't believe what I was hearing. All the girls looked at me like, *Is she actually starting?* I had taken an All-American player's starting spot and I could tell she was livid. But I had worked hard to get to that position, so I didn't give a damn who didn't like it.

Before we walked out to the court, I went up to Coach and said, "I got you, Boo." And as soon as we started playing, all my jitters went out the window. I was in the zone, hitting three-pointers one after another. I was getting more buckets than I normally did.

We won, and at the end of that game I found out I'd scored forty points. I had never scored forty in my entire basketball career.

The next game was later that day, so we went to get something to eat before it started. After eating quickly, I would usually find somewhere to lie down so I could rejuvenate for the next game. Following a quick nap, I was more than ready.

Now that I was a starter, the pressure was on to make even more buckets—I didn't want to have my spot taken away. I could see more college coaches in the stands, and while I knew they weren't there for me, I still played my best.

I had another forty-point game, and the coaching staff just couldn't believe it. *I* couldn't believe it! There was no way I was coming out of the starting lineup now. Nobody else's stats on the team were even close to mine.

I had forty-plus points in each game leading up to the championship. By the time we got to the final game, however, I had a big, raw blister on the bottom of my foot that made it nearly impossible to play. But I wasn't letting nothing stop me from playing—not some stupid blister, anyway. The staff helped me wrap it, but during warm-ups I could feel it burning like hell.

The buzzer went off for us to start, and I looked up to see a packed gym, with college coaches and plenty of the other players from the teams who hadn't made it to the championship game. I was anxious to get the show on the road, but at the same time, that blister was killing me. I couldn't even run after I scored my first two points of the game. So I yelled over, "Boo, I need a sub!"

As I limped to the bench, Boo greeted me, "N-n-n-now, n-n-now, Sugar, what's wrong?" Boo was always stuttering, but I'd never had a problem understanding him because DD Bug stuttered too.

"This blister is killing me!"

He didn't say nothing in response, just continued to coach. I was irritated—I couldn't believe a stupid blister was keeping me from playing. I sat on the bench for the remainder of the game, watching my teammates win.

Afterward, it was time to name the first team of the tournament and to announce the MVP of the game. In my mind there was no way I was winning MVP since I hadn't even played the full championship game.

They started by naming first team. I wasn't called—it was girls from the other team and two from mine. I was pissed I didn't get first team. But I always showed good sportsmanship, so I clapped loudly. Inside, I was mad as hell. When the two girls from my team returned to the bench, they didn't even seem that happy that they'd made first team.

And then over the loudspeaker I heard, "*The most valuable player award goes to Sugar Rodgers.*"

My first thought was that they'd made a mistake. I didn't realize MVP was based on the whole tournament, not just the championship game.

I walked up to accept the MVP trophy, smiling ear to ear. I was so proud. I didn't even realize it until later, but my cousin Keda's husband, Maurice, was there to see me play. I was so touched that there had been someone in the stands rooting just for *me*!

I called my friends and family back home to let them know I won MVP. Everybody was happy for me, especially Kakie. She loved to hear me in good spirits, especially since she'd known how hard it had been for me with the death of my mother. I dedicated that MVP trophy to my mother.

CHAPTER 18

GETTING RECRUITED

ALMOST EVERY TOURNAMENT AFTER THAT, I started and we won. It felt like we were unbeatable until we went to a tournament in Philly and ended up losing a couple of games that we were supposed to win.

Back at the hotel, the team captains called a meeting. Before it started, they said we were going to go around and say something about each teammate, whether it was good or bad. We sat down in a circle, and the girl sitting right across from me was selected to start. I had a bad feeling about this exercise, though I just sat there quietly.

The girl pointed straight at me and started saying some crazy stuff. Then she stood up like she was about to hit me. I stood up too and said, "You don't wanna do that." As she approached me, two other girls from the team grabbed hold of my arms.

"Let me go!" I shouted, slamming both of them onto a nearby bed. I didn't mean no harm, I just don't like people grabbing me when I'm about to fight. They understood where I was coming from. They were like, "Calm down, Sugar."

"I *am* calm, just don't grab me."

The girl was still shouting crazy stuff at me, and finally a few of my teammates managed to get her out of there and I went back to my own room. But I had been ready for that fight. I liked fighting; that's all we ever did in the hood.

After this incident, and since we were losing games we should have been winning, Boo decided to pull us out of the tournament.

That summer I received a bunch of college letters in the mail—so many coaches were offering me scholarships. I was amazed because college had never been something I'd focused on much at all. I always assumed I'd join the army after high school.

Where I'm from, college was frowned upon—you either dropped out of high school and hit the streets; got pregnant and then dropped out; went to jail; enlisted in the army; or you got killed. Graduating high school had always been my only academic goal.

But once those offers started pouring in, I put more effort towards doing well in both school and basketball, because now I realized I wanted to go to college. Even before playing with Boo, there had been one college that had caught my attention, and that was Georgetown.

Georgetown coaches had seen me play early on in high school when they were at a game recruiting a girl from my same district. After that, the Georgetown coaching staff would check in with me from time to time. I didn't take the attention seriously, however, because I simply couldn't picture myself going there, plus their basketball team sucked. But I remember Boo saying after one of our wins that he thought I'd end up playing college ball there.

Come to find out, Boo's sister Terri was the head coach at Georgetown. Now I knew why he wanted me to go to there: his sister would take good care of me just like he had.

Boo wasn't just a great coach to me. There were plenty of times I couldn't find a ride to practice and he would send somebody to come get me. I had been on plenty of trips with Boo with no money in my pocket, and he always made sure I ate. He knew the struggle was real for me, so he wanted to be sure I was surrounded by good people if I went away to college.

So, Georgetown quickly became my first and last pick. It wasn't just that Boo's sister Terri was there; the school had been interested in me even before I started getting buckets on that elite level.

I was introduced to the coaching staff for the first time up at Georgetown during a tournament. There was a tall, skinny lady with a long weave, a light-skinned pretty boy, and a big, loudmouthed black guy who always came to see me play.

One talent I had developed from my childhood was reading people. The tall lady with the long weave gave me a bad vibe. I remember there was one time she came to one of my games and told my coaches I wasn't Georgetown-ready because I'd only scored fifteen points. It had just been an off night for me.

The next game was a couple days later and the loudmouthed black guy was there to see me play. He was my favorite because I could talk trash to him like a dude in the streets. I scored fifty points in that game, and asked him to pass along a message to his coworker with the weave: "Tell her I do this for a living."

I felt comfortable talking trash with that man, yet I didn't talk hardly at all to the rest of the coaching staff who came to see me over the years.

CHAPTER 19

POWDER PUFF

IT WAS MY HIGH SCHOOL POWDER PUFF GAME, where the boys dressed up as cheerleaders, making noise on the sidelines, and the girls played flag football on the field. I was excited because I had always loved playing football. The game was the eleventh graders versus the twelfth graders, so Ransheda and I were on different teams and ended up both being quarterbacks. Winning this game would give the eleventh grade bragging rights for the rest of the year.

It was spirit week, and at the pep rally earlier in the week the school had encouraged everyone to come out for the powder puff game. Most people had planned on coming anyway.

The day of the game, school let out early and I went home to grab something to eat and take a quick nap. When we got back to school that night, we suited up and took the field like a real football team. A coin was flipped and my team picked heads, but it came up tails. The twelfth graders chose to receive, and the announcer said, "Let the game begin!"

It was pretty intense and the score was really

close throughout the game, until the twelfth graders went up by two touchdowns with time running out. So the seniors ended up winning, but we all had a lot of fun.

As She-She and I were leaving, we saw a girl she knew standing near the exit crying. The girl told us that another girl had been picking on her. She-She went right over to confront the bully. I followed her to make sure nothing was going to pop off. But before I knew it, She-She and the bully were squared off, ready to fight. I was trying to hold my best friend back, but once the other girl started swinging, I let go.

Then the bully's cousin snuck up and popped me in the face. I was taught that if you hit me, I will hit you back. So I went off, swinging punches. Then I grabbed her, picked her up over my head, and slammed her down on her back. I got on top of her and started hitting her in the face.

At this point, everything was pretty much a blur and I was barely conscious of what I was doing. But eventually reality set in. I could see She-She and my cousin Keda running towards me, and behind them I noticed several cops hurrying in our direction.

I hopped off the girl and sprinted towards Keda's car. Once we got inside, Keda snapped, "What the hell happened?"

I started talking out of breath, all jittery from the fight: "She, she went over th-there to t-talk to that girl and then they just started fighting. Before I knew what was h-happening, that other girl punched me in the face. So then I started f-fighting."

Keda dropped me off at my aunt's, and as soon as I walked in, I announced, "Aunt Linda, I got in a fight. A girl punched me in the face, and then we started fighting. Tomorrow when I go to school, they said I'm gonna get suspended for ten days."

She asked how the fight started and I told her. My aunt listened, and decided not to punish me. She said she understood that I was defending myself. After we finished talking, I called Kakie and told her what had happened.

The next day, as soon as I got to school, I was sent straight to the principal's office, where I received my ten-day suspension, which would be followed by an administrative hearing where the school board would determine whether or not they should let me back.

But that wasn't even the worst of it. Come to find out, the other girl's parents were pressing charges against She-She and me.

I told my aunt all the bad news as soon as I got back home. And a couple days later, I received the court date in the mail. Things were getting ugly.

We ended up having a hearing at the courthouse. She-She and I had to each do twenty-five hours of community service, and I had to write an apology letter to the girl I beat up.

Going to basketball practice after school somehow qualified as community service, so that was easy, and the letter I wrote was simple too—just a few sentences saying how sorry I was. But I wasn't really, because she'd hit me first. That's just how I was raised.

The girl's parents wanted me kicked out of school for the rest of the year and said the school was showing favoritism because I was a basketball player. They were even more mad because their daughter was embarrassed to go back to school. Turned out that I had slammed her so hard she pissed all over herself. But if their daughter would've kept her hands to herself, we wouldn't have ended up in this mess.

I was glad when it was all over because I had a lot to lose. If I had gotten kicked out of school, I would have lost my scholarship. I would've messed up my junior year and my basketball season. Luckily, I didn't lose anything. I was on track and more focused than ever from that point forward.

There was one more thing I wanted to do as a high school basketball player: compete in the McDonalds's All-American game in Miami, Florida. I told Boo about this dream, and in exchange for him helping me, I had to do better in school. So every day after school for about two weeks, I stayed behind to make up work and earn some extra credit. I would go to school late, but at least I was going. Soon I could see things getting better as my attitude towards school improved. Boo and an assistant coach from Georgetown named Brown had a meeting with the administrators and encouraged my teachers to help me help myself.

Before I knew it, I received a letter in the mail saying I'd been nominated to play in the game. Nobody from my city had ever been selected for this game, but I knew everybody watched it. The summer between ninth and tenth grade I had worked at McDonald's, making $7.50 an hour. In almost no time at all, I had gone from flipping burgers at McDonald's to being a McDonald's All-American. It was an unbelievable feeling and an absolute honor to be chosen.

I only had two audience tickets so it was really hard to decide who to invite to the game. Sharon had recently gotten out of prison and I thought she might want to go, but I wasn't really sure. DD Bug and my oldest nephew, Vanshawn, were both currently in jail so they were out of the question. Of course, Kakie was the first person I offered a ticket to, but she didn't have the money to make the trip. Sharon got upset that I didn't invite her, but to be honest, I didn't think she liked basketball very much. So I ended up inviting my coaches Keda and Betty.

As it turned out, a lot of people from the hood watched the game and it was a lot of fun. Even my nephew Scooter surprised me by showing up. It was the first time he'd even been on an airplane—he'd barely left Suffolk before. He and I took a walk down the Miami strip, joking around and sightseeing. I knew this would be a great memory I would cherish for a long time.

CHAPTER 20

SENIOR PROM

EVERY YEAR OF HIGH SCHOOL, I was invited to prom. And I denied every guy who asked me. Guys from other schools asked me as well, but it was always a no-go. I had no interest in going to prom. All you did was dress up and take pictures.

I was able to avoid prom for my first three years of high school, despite Kakie's nagging that I should go. But my senior year was different.

"Aunt Sugar, you going this year? You're a senior, it's only right! I'm gonna make sure you look good, Auntie!"

"Kakie," I sighed, "I'm not sure if I really want to go."

"Girl, you *have* to go. I can't wait to see you in a dress!"

While I still wasn't that excited about the idea of dressing up for prom, I finally decided maybe she was right. But I sure didn't want to waste my money on a dress and heels when I could spend it on some new J's.

So I told Kakie I'd go, but she would have to find

me a dress and heels. I wasn't much looking forward to putting on makeup and getting my hair done either, as I preferred my natural look. But when it came to dressing up, I always left this all up to Kakie because she had a great sense of fashion.

As promised, she did find a dress for me to wear, and one night she picked me up and brought me over to her place to check it out.

"Do you like it, Aunt Sugar?" she asked as she pulled a beautiful dress out of her closet.

"I love it!"

"I knew you would. Try it on."

I hopped out of my basketball shorts and T-shirt and pulled the dress over my head.

"Damn," said Kakie. "Damn . . . girl, you are beautiful. That dress hugs every curve!"

I smiled back. "Thank you, Kakie! But how much was it? This dress looks expensive."

"Girl," Kakie replied with a sly smile on her face, "you know I stole that dress. I couldn't let you go to prom looking any kind of way except perfect."

I just shook my head and thought to myself, *How the fuck do you steal a whole prom dress?*

After a long week of school, Friday finally came. I took a half day off school, and Kakie picked me up early so I could get ready for prom.

First, I went to a salon to get my nails and toes done. Then we went to another salon to get my hair done, though Kakie didn't like how it came out so she took me to some girl's house to fix it.

After that she took me home, and Keda brought me over to her friend's place to get my makeup done. By the time we were finished with all this running around, I only had a few minutes to get dressed.

Once I was ready, I went outside to take pictures with my family and friends. It seemed like everyone and their mom came to see my off. They all stood around complimenting me, saying, "Awww . . . you look so cute!"

"*Awwwww,*" She-She said with a smirk on her face, "*aren't you so cute. If only you had taken Tone to prom . . .*"

I rolled my eyes but I knew she was teasing me. Tone was a guy I'd dated in high school, but I didn't want to go to prom with him. Honestly, I wanted to go by myself and didn't have any interest in taking a date. Plus, my cousin BeBe was going without a date as well, and I knew we'd have more fun together.

I took so many pictures with friends and family and, oh yeah, I can't forget about my boyfriend Spalding the basketball—we took a few photos with "him" as well!

Keda's husband, Maurice, let me take his brand-new car. As he handed me the keys, he said, "Don't be hitting the gas too hard, and be safe!"

"I will, I promise! And thank you, Maurice!"

I hopped into the car and drove off to pick up

BeBe. We spent a few minutes at her place taking more photos with her family and then we were off to prom.

Most everyone was surprised I went that year, and even more surprised to see me all dressed up— everyone was so used to seeing me in my basketball gear.

But even though I'd agreed to go, my plan was to get in and get out. So as soon as we got there, BeBe and I headed over to get our official prom photos taken. The line was really long and the high heels were killing my feet. We finally got to the front of the line and BeBe went first, then it was my turn.

"One, two, three, *cheese!*" the cameraman said before snapping some photos, and just like that prom was over for me. I was out!

It wasn't just prom that I was dodging. Even though I did date a bit, I didn't have much of a romantic life. I was too focused on basketball, and with all the other drama in my life, I was busy trying to survive. Having a boyfriend just wasn't that important to me.

CHAPTER 21

GEORGETOWN HOYAS

SO I PLAYED IN THE McDONALD'S All-American game like they had promised me. Now it was time to get ready for college at Georgetown.

High school graduation day was an enjoyable time for me, because I was able to see all the various people who'd been supporting me since day one. Kakie, Keda, and She-She were particularly excited for me because neither had been able to attend her own graduation—Kakie had actually given birth on the day of her graduation.

Everybody who came was so proud to see me accomplish something that I, at one point, hadn't thought was possible. That summer flew by, and before I knew it I was packing my bags to head off to college. As someone on a basketball scholarship, I had to spend an extra month down there before school started, and participate in something they called the "scholars program," where I'd meet the other players and get familiar with Georgetown.

Once I arrived on campus, the coaches checked me in and showed me to my dorm. Keda and her husband, Maurice, helped me move all my stuff in before they said their goodbyes.

The campus was beautiful. To me, it looked like something out of a Harry Potter movie. In general, I wasn't usually a fan of getting to know new people, but I realized this was an opportunity to better my future and set an example for others.

After being there only a couple of hours, however, I was nearly ready to go home. People were *too* nice; the talk *so* proper. They were too friendly and I wasn't used to that; it made me feel uncomfortable.

Yet I didn't leave, and after the first couple weeks I got to know a few of my fellow students, though none were on the basketball team. I had convinced myself that I didn't like my teammates. I didn't even know them, of course, but they were different.

After one practice, I said to my coach: "Coach Brown, let me just go home for the month. Then I'll come back."

He laughed. "Sugar, I can't let you do that, but everything will be okay. Just give it a chance. Get to know some people. Matter of fact, I got somebody I want to introduce you to right now . . . Coach Thompson."

I had heard so much about the legendary Coach John Thompson of the Hoyas men's team and I was finally going to meet him. He was huge, nearly seven feet and 250-plus pounds. Solid. You always knew when he was in the gym, because he would be there

in a big wooden chair that everyone else was for-
bidden to sit in. It was sort of like his throne. I had
heard so many great things about him and his history at Georgetown that I was nervous to meet him.
I'd also heard he either liked you or he didn't—there
wasn't no in-between.

Coach Brown called me over: "This is Sugar
Rodgers, the player I told you about."

"Hey, Coach Thompson, nice to meet you," I
greeted.

"Nice to meet you too, Sugar," he said. "I've
heard so many great things about you. Can you play
like they say you can?"

I'm thinking to myself, *Is this a trick question?*
But I went ahead and responded, "I *can* play!"

"How you liking Georgetown so far?"

I hesitated before responding, "It's okay so far, I
guess."

"You guess?"

"It's okay," I repeated.

Coach Brown walked off and left us alone for a
few minutes. Coach Thompson offered me the open
chair right next to him. I sat down and we continued talking in the empty gym. The way he spoke,
you could tell he was a wise man. He put you in the
eyes of a grandfather, but he also reminded me of
my own father. He began sharing knowledge about
Georgetown and about life that gave me a new
perspective—but I still wanted to go home.

From that point on, every time Coach Thompson was in the gym, I would go over and pick his brain.

So I stayed until the scholars program was over. Unsurprisingly, I hated when the professors made me read out loud. The few times I tried, I found myself stuttering and stumbling over words I knew. I would go from simple embarrassment to judging myself harshly—my hands would start sweating and my body would feel hot all over. Eventually, whenever I was called on, I would either refuse to speak or simply say I couldn't read. That wasn't true—I *could* read! But it just made me way too nervous. I also avoided raising my hand to participate in class discussions.

Honestly, that program almost scared me away from college altogether. It was challenging, but I stuck with it and made it through. Even though I'd already been through a lot of changes, this was the biggest transition of my life.

I had two weeks off between the scholars program and the start of regular classes at Georgetown, and I spent those back home with my family. I was the first in my family to go to college and I remember telling my nephew Scooter that he'd better be at every basketball game.

"You already know, Auntie," he replied, with his pretty smile and deep dimples. Even though I was younger than he was, he still called me *Auntie*. To some people it was weird, but for us it was the norm.

* * *

One thing about my siblings is that they loved to party. I didn't like to party, so I'd stay home and babysit my great-nieces and great-nephews. I mostly avoided parties and socials because people got too drunk and started fighting. Seemed like every party or social ended with gunshots.

Like this one social Kakie put together for me right before I went back to Georgetown: some guys started arguing over something, and as soon as one guy reached in his pants, the others were like, "Oh, shit, he got a gun." I could see people scattering like roaches. I crouched down low and ran behind the building. I could hear the bullets flying past me as I lay on the ground. I'm thinking to myself, *Who brought a machine gun to the party?* It was like World War III out there.

Once the shooting died down, everybody took off in his or her car, and I could hear the police sirens coming from a mile away. In my neighborhood, there was only one way in and one way out.

She-She and I ran to Kakie's house. Kakie had organized the social as a way to raise some pocket money for me. Even though I had a full scholarship, she wanted to make sure I had some spending money.

But like I said, too many parties ended in gunshots, and that one was no exception. That night one person got shot (and a few cars), but no one died.

The guy who got shot was actually kind of lucky—most shootings in my hood ended with at least one person dead.

CHAPTER 22

SCOOTER

::

IT WAS AUGUST 23, 2009, the day before I was supposed to head back to college. After I finished packing at Keda's house, I went over to Kakie's to see my great-nieces and -nephews and say goodbye.

"Auntie Sugar will be heading off to college, so y'all be good for your mother and dad, okay?" I said.

And then came all the questions:

"What's college?"

"When you coming back?"

"Who you staying with?"

"Can *we* go?"

I didn't quite know how to explain college to a bunch of little kids, especially since no one else in their world had ever talked much about it.

I kept it simple and just said, "Auntie Sugar got a scholarship to play basketball at a university." They nodded their heads like they knew what a scholarship was.

Then we all went outside and played until it got dark. I had already planned to spend the night at Kakie's, and after the kids and I were done playing,

Kakie said, "Hey, Auntie Sugar, can you watch the children?"

"Where you going?" I asked.

"I'm going to a party," she said, while starting to get dressed.

I knew there was a party in the city, because my nephew Scooter had stopped by Kakie's on his way there. Before I let him leave I'd said, "Let me get some money, Scooter, 'cause I'm off to college tomorrow."

As he gave me fifty dollars in five-dollar bills, he said, "You better do big things, Auntie."

"You already know," I replied.

Once Kakie left, I popped in a movie to watch with the kids before bedtime.

Boom boom!

"Open the door! Scooter's been in a car accident!" some guy from the neighborhood shouted.

I jumped off the couch where I'd fallen asleep and opened the front door. My heart was pounding out of my chest. Then the guy turned around and took off running up the street. I guessed he was heading back to the scene of the accident.

It was like five in the morning. I called Kakie first, but there was no answer, so then I called my sister. No answer. I called everyone I could think of—nobody was picking up their phones. I started to seriously panic, slowly realizing that something could really be wrong.

All of a sudden, a car pulls up in front of Kakie's, and I hear, "Sugar, Sugar, Scooter dead!" My niece was screaming and crying as she jumped out of the vehicle with Sharon close behind her.

I was in an immediate state of shock as I ran outside to comfort them.

"My brother dead, my baby brother dead!" Kakie kept repeating. By this time, it seemed like the whole city knew. People from all over the neighborhood started pulling up in front of Kakie's house. Everybody was in tears—well, everyone except for me because I was still in shock.

Scooter had a young son with one girl and another baby boy on the way with another girl. I was thinking, *Who's going to help take care of them? It's hard being a single parent.* Then I thought, *Who's going to tell Vanshawn and DD Bug in jail?*

Sharon was going crazy with rage and Kakie couldn't stop crying.

Shit got more real (if that's even possible) when I had to tell my great-nephew Mo that his favorite uncle had passed away. He burst out crying and then Kakie, who had stopped her tears for a few minutes, started weeping again. I just sat there numbly watching Kakie comfort Mo.

I called a couple family members to let them know what was going on and talk about what we had to do next. Sharon took on a lot of the planning—she had to find money to pay for the funeral. She also had to contact the jail to see if DD Bug and Vanshawn would be allowed out to attend the funeral. Then she had to go down to the morgue to identify the body. The lady told Sharon that Scooter had died immediately from the impact that broke his spine. There was a lot to do in a short amount of time, and after briefly falling apart the night Scooter died, Sharon got herself together quickly to deal with it all.

I of course delayed my return to Georgetown. The whole week I was trying to keep it together too. I didn't cry at the viewing. I just couldn't believe that this was my nephew lying in the casket. Fortunately, the funeral service went very well. We had all turned up for Scooter. It's what he would have wanted. By the time the funeral was nearly over, however, I was done holding myself together. I went up to his casket one last time and gave him a kiss on his cold cheek.

And then, when I made it out to the church parking lot, I finally broke down. I couldn't face the fact that my nephew was gone forever. The nephew I'd taught how to shoot dice; the nephew who'd made me get hit by a car; the nephew my mother and I went to get when he broke out of the boys' home he was living in; the nephew who always gave me hugs and kisses; the nephew who made me feel loved; the nephew who never let me down; the nephew I loved like a brother.

Scooter was gone forever.

CHAPTER 23

FRESHMAN YEAR

TWO DAYS AFTER SCOOTER'S FUNERAL SERVICE I started my freshman year of college. In order not to lose my scholarship, I had to rush back, giving me no time to mourn.

I'd missed freshman orientation, so after I unpacked, I went over to my academic advisor's office to pick up my class schedule and a list of books I'd need. Luckily, since I'd been there for the scholars program I knew where most things were on campus.

The first day of classes, I couldn't believe how much homework I already had. I'd never read three chapters or typed a five-page paper in such a short amount of time. I was completely overwhelmed, but instead of asking for help I just didn't do it.

On top of all the schoolwork, it was preseason, and we were training really hard. The coaches decided we needed to be able to run a mile in six minutes and forty-five seconds. I had never run a mile that fast. We started practice early, meeting at the track to start timing our runs. I was sure there was no way

I'd make it. I hadn't trained for this. I'd been doing basketball stuff.

Ready . . . set . . . go!

I tried to keep up but kept falling behind. At least I didn't come in last—I came in next-to-last. Since I didn't make the mile, I had to go to "Hell Week," plus still do all the required daily exercises. And on top of that, I still had to attend classes. I wasn't ready for all this.

Hell Week was the worst part of the season. I had to wake up at 4:30 a.m. to run for two hours every day for a whole week. The first day I thought I was going to die. After running, I went to class and promptly fell asleep.

And it wasn't just the morning runs, there was conditioning too. Mind you, I couldn't even find time to eat because when I wasn't running or training, I was sleeping. Come to find out, my coaches' definition of conditioning was just more running with no basketball. I was pissed.

One day during Hell Week, after a couple of suicides and "33" (which were suicides with a back padding), I plopped down on the ground and said, "I'm not running no more. I didn't sign up to be on the damn track team!"

One of my teammates, a senior, said, "Sugar, get up and just keep running."

So I got up and kept running, even though I wasn't making the times—I just kept pushing.

* * *

Once preseason was over, practice got easier. Until, of course, somebody got in trouble for not going to class. Usually that somebody was me.

For the first three weeks of college, I didn't do any of my schoolwork. My professors e-mailed my academic advisor, who then told my coaches. My coaches and I had a meeting and I told them how much I hated school. I told them I was tired and I didn't know how to do it. I finally admitted I needed some help. I didn't know how to manage my time with so many things going on, and all I really wanted to do was play basketball.

My coaches jumped into action, and by the middle of the semester I had a tutor for every subject. Without them tutors, I probably would've failed my first semester.

With my schoolwork somewhat under control, I could really focus on what I loved—playing ball.

November 14, 2009, was my first college game— an away game at Missouri State. I was excited and also motivated by all the work I had put in. I wasn't just doing better academically, my basketball work ethic had also improved. Monica McNutt, a junior on the team who'd taken me under her wing, was making sure I did all my schoolwork and didn't start falling behind again. She was hard on me and made sure I went to class. In between classes, we'd go to the gym. In fact, we worked out every day, staying after practice for extra training, weight lifting, etc.

If Moni found out I'd skipped a meal, she'd bring me a sandwich. I spent countless hours in the gym with her and Corey, the pretty-boy assistant coach. He would teach us something new every day, pushing us both to the max.

I soon realized, after all these hours working out, that it was becoming fun. I was actually enjoying it. I was eating better, and I was getting stronger, building up my muscle mass—my body and mind were doing a 180. Only Moni and the assistant coach were aware of how hard I was training, but when it was time for the lights to come on, I knew all my hard work would show, and I really hoped it would pay off. I'd never imagined myself making it this far—a starting freshman on the Georgetown Hoyas! I was pleased with myself, though I wanted more.

So, by that first game at Missouri State, I was ready. Since we were the away team, the announcer called us first. I was sitting on the bench waiting to be called, when I heard, *"Georgetown, number fourteen, Ta'Shauna Rodgers."*

I sat there for a few seconds before I got up and ran over to join my team. My coaches assumed I was nervous and that's why I hadn't jumped up immediately. But that wasn't why I'd hesitated. After we broke it down as a team, I turned to Coach Brown and explained what had happened: "Nobody calls me by my government name."

He simply said, "Ain't nobody calling *Sugar*."

"Okay," I responded, knowing it was time to focus on the game, and not on what name they'd announced over the loudspeaker.

We won, 79–55. I scored twenty-one points and grabbed five rebounds. I approached Coach Brown after the game and said, "They better call me Sugar now." And before you knew it, everybody was calling me Sugar.

After that first game, and for the rest of the season, plenty of journalists wanted to interview me, but I didn't want to talk to the media. I didn't like the spotlight, plus I didn't talk proper like my teammates. Not only did I use slang from the streets I'd grown up on, I also distrusted the media. I knew they could manipulate you into saying something you might not even mean, or portray you as something you're not. When I was back home, the news had done that to my nephew one time, saying he had murdered a girl when he hadn't—so I knew what the media was capable of.

My first college season, I ended up winning rookie of the week nearly every other week. In the Big East Conference, I was named rookie of the year! And when I made the All-Big East's first team as a freshman, that was the first time I realized I had a real chance to make it to the WNBA.

CHAPTER 24

DAD

BY MY SECOND YEAR OF COLLEGE, I was walking around campus without a care in the world, thoroughly enjoying school. Classes were going well, and I managed to maintain a 3.0 grade point average for both semesters. But still, I knew shit was always going on back home. I felt like it was time for me to let go of my past. I wanted to move forward to a new future that was opening up for me. It was a make-or-break situation for me—I was either going to make it through college or drop out.

My family was struggling so I knew I had to make it. Thoughts of home stressed me out—I wanted to always be there for my family and help them out in any way I could, yet I didn't want to mess up my future.

Just like freshman year, I went to the gym all the time, though I was in a different headspace. When Coach Brown asked me what was wrong I would confide in him, share my worries.

"Sugar, you can't control what's going on at home," he would say to me.

I knew I couldn't control it, but I figured I could help. When he suggested that I go to counseling, seek out professional help to manage my stress and anxiety, I said, "Coach Brown, that's for white people. Do I look like someone who's going to talk to some white guy about my problems? Nine times out of ten, he ain't gonna be able to relate."

"Sugar, counseling's for everybody. Everybody needs someone to talk to."

But I was stuck in a hood mentality when it came to therapy. Stuck, that was, until I found myself so depressed I was barely leaving my room. So I finally gave in and went. I told myself it couldn't hurt to give it a try.

The first time I walked into the therapist's waiting room, I felt weird and uncomfortable. I felt like everyone there was staring at me, like I was crazy or something. But they weren't even thinking about me. I quickly realized they had their own problems and they weren't paying me any attention.

My first session ran over two hours. I just sat there and cried. I cried until my head starting hurting and the veins in my forehead were popping out. Eventually, once I stopped sobbing, we started talking about my life. At first, I wasn't very open; I wasn't used to talking to strangers about things from my childhood, my past.

But I kept going to counseling every week, and slowly I began opening up more and more—venting about all my problems from the past, from back home. One day I got so deep about what had happened in my life, my counselor started crying too.

I realized I actually enjoyed going to counseling. After each session, I felt free.

While I was dealing with my depression and figuring out how to move forward with my life, my commitment to basketball was getting inconsistent. I was in and out of love with the game all sophomore year.

Regardless of my feelings, early in the season I received an invitation to the USA World University Team tryouts. Instead of training harder to get ready for the tryouts, however, I decided to go home to visit my family. During this time, while I was digging deep during my counseling sessions, I felt like I needed to see them more than ever because so many of my family members had already died. If somebody from home called me a few times, I'd immediately go into panic mode and think the worst—that someone else had passed away. From a young age, I had learned the hard truth that tomorrow isn't a guarantee for everyone. So I cherished the family I did have left.

After a good visit home, I returned to school in time to fly out to Colorado for the USA World University Team tryouts. They went okay for me, though my playing was far from my best. But in a way it almost didn't matter how well I played; we all knew it was political. I mean, it seemed pretty crazy to me that the assistant coach for the team I was trying out for was the sister of Boo, Georgetown's head coach.

At the end of the last tryout, they announced the players who had made the team. My name wasn't called. It was my first time getting cut. I was mad at myself because I hadn't taken advantage of this amazing opportunity. I knew I'd messed up, and the only thing I could do now was return to the gym and start working harder than ever.

Sometimes, just when you think things can't get any worse, they do. Throughout the year, my father's health had been declining. I had been in close contact with him, but as he grew sicker and sicker, I received fewer and fewer calls. I stayed in touch with my siblings to make sure I was up-to-date on what was going on, and eventually they told me I should come back home to see him. My father wasn't doing well and no one knew how much longer he'd survive. So I took that three-hour trip back to visit him. And they were right: he was barely holding on. His memory was in and out, but as soon as I walked into the room he knew exactly who I was. All I could do was stare at my father's face. By this point in my life, I knew what death looked like, and my father looked just like my mother had in her final days.

A couple days after returning to school from the visit, I got the call that my father had passed away.

CHAPTER 25

SENIOR YEAR

SENIOR YEAR WAS A WALK IN THE PARK. I had done everything necessary to graduate on time, and by my final year, I only had five classes left to take. I took four in the first semester, leaving me with one class for my last semester.

I added a work-study program to my schedule, under the guidance of one of my favorite professors, Monica Maxwell-Paegle. I had told her that writing stuff down had a therapeutic effect on me, so the focus of my work-study program shifted to writing.

It was a new start for our team as well because Brown had been named head coach. Changing coaches could go one of two ways—bad or good. I was excited that Coach Brown got the job. Because we players were already comfortable with him as a coach, it meant there wouldn't be tons of new changes. Plus, Coach Brown knew what each player was capable of.

Unfortunately, our season didn't go very well. Several players got injured along the way, so there was just more and more pressure on the team. Every game, I faced a box and one, where one player guarded me everywhere I went. It was frustrating, but it also showed that my opponents knew that I was a threat. They knew that if they kept on me the whole game, they'd have a chance at winning.

I was a silent assassin on the court, and although I never talked trash, I was gritty. I played with a chip on my shoulder; I was physical and could shoot the three ball from anywhere—and I mean *anywhere*. I had earned the go-go green light and would fill up the stat sheet every night.

The team my senior year was young and inexperienced—most of my fellow teammates hadn't played at such a high level and were learning the game in real time. I was confident in my young team—I remembered what it was like to be inexperienced—but it wasn't enough for me to be confident: they needed to have confidence in themselves, which was something that many of them lacked.

While we didn't make it to the NCAA tournament at the end of the season, I personally had a decent season. I broke the Hoyas' all-time scoring record of 2,304 points that was held by Sleepy Floyd. I scored 2,518 points that year, breaking Floyd's thirty-one-year record from 1982. I had broken a lot of records, but this one meant a lot to me because there had been so many great players who came through Georgetown over the years.

By the time April rolled around, I was ready to

graduate—something nobody in my family had ever done, something people told me I would never accomplish, and something that brought me and my family together for another great moment.

But as I'd come to learn, it never fails—when something good happens, something bad is inevitably just around the corner. Shortly before graduation, I got a terrible call that Aunt Linda had passed away. It seemed like every year somebody else in my family died.

CHAPTER 26

PREPARING FOR THE PROS

COLLEGE WAS OVER NOW—it was time for me to get ready for the pros. As soon as my coaches knew I was serious about wanting to play in the WNBA, they came up with a plan to get me there. They also knew how important it was to help me stay on track, explaining that there would be certain sacrifices I would need to make, certain things I wouldn't be able to do if I was serious about making it to the WNBA.

Of course, by this time I was already used to giving up certain things. All throughout my college years, I had spent part of every summer taking extra classes at Georgetown so my load during the semester wouldn't be too heavy, allowing me to focus as much as possible on basketball. And after the first summer, I had realized I actually wanted to stay at school in DC, even though it meant missing out on seeing my friends and family. Whenever I did make it home, something crazy would happen—someone would get shot at or a fistfight would break out. When I was back home, I was always worried about being in the wrong place at the wrong time. Seemed to me like nothing positive was going on back home anyway.

Ultimately, my degree was worth more to me than going to the pros because nobody could take away my knowledge. I knew when it came to playing basketball, I could easily get hurt and it could all be over, just like that. So I wasn't going to sacrifice my degree, but luckily I didn't need to sacrifice playing basketball either.

CHAPTER 27

DRAFT DAY

AS THE WNBA DRAFT APPROACHED, I was ready for it. I was projected as a top-five pick, and I really wanted to go to the Washington Mystics so I could stay in DC and still be pretty close to home.

I had been working very hard. I had decided to stay with Hanif, the trainer I'd worked out with the previous summer. And during my senior year, when it became clear the Hoyas weren't making it to the NCAA tournament, I started training constantly, without taking any days off. After team practice, I would go work out more with Coach Valentine, one of my Georgetown coaches. We focused on a lot of different things and he showed me where I would get my shots from. Most importantly, he made sure I had the moves to *create* my own shots. Working on those moves over and over and over ensured that I had the skills down tight. Once I got a certain move down, I would then do it at game speed against Hanif. I hated when somebody took the ball from me, and he would do this often.

Hanif was a great trainer. He had worked with

some big-time NBA players, so I knew he would get me ready. He pushed me to my fullest potential and brought out the best in me.

I also needed to find an agent if I wanted to have a pro career. Unlike the process of identifying my trainer, figuring out who to hire as my agent was a different situation and much more complicated. I don't play when it comes to my money—either you get the job done or you don't. I interviewed a couple of agents before finally identifying one I felt I could trust with my career. I especially wanted my agent's help with finding me a good team to join overseas, which is where most players competed after the WNBA season ended.

The night before I left for the draft, which was being held at the ESPN offices near Hartford, Connecticut, I went out to eat with my teammate Katie McCormick. We talked and laughed and had a great time.

At one point Katie said, "Sugar, it doesn't matter how high or low you go, at least you going. Most people don't get these opportunities."

She was exactly right. Most people didn't get this type of opportunity. I knew this, but hearing Katie say it really helped. I went into the draft with the mentality that it didn't matter how high or low I went. I was just determined to enjoy the moment.

Coach Brown brought me to the airport and I checked in two hours early. Then, just as I sat down at my gate, an announcement was made saying the flight was delayed due to bad weather. After another hour, the flight was canceled.

I called the WNBA staff and fortunately they were able to find me another way to get to Connecticut. Since my bags had already been sent ahead on another plane, arrangements were made for someone from the WNBA to pick them up for me. Then they sent a car to collect me at the airport outside of DC and take me to Union Station. I arrived just before my train was scheduled to depart.

It was a six-hour train ride to Hartford, Connecticut. I spent most of the time texting and talking on the phone, and before I knew it we were there. It was around midnight and I'd missed all the rookie meetings that day, but I'd made it.

There were more meetings the following day—some were productive, others were just time-consuming. But it was nice to see some of the girls I'd played against over the years, and there was a players panel that I really enjoyed—it was deep and emotional.

I couldn't wait for my family to arrive. In addition to my sister, brother, and niece, who were all coming, I'd also invited Coach Brown and Boo's sister Terri. This was going to be the first time in about eleven years that my brother, sister, and I would all be in the same room together. DD Bug had just gotten out of prison, so he was incredibly excited to see me. (When Coach Brown heard that my brother was having trouble coming up with the cash to travel to the draft, he made sure DD Bug would be there.)

Even though my brother and sister had been in and out my life, it was important to me that they be there because their mistakes and sacrifices had helped me to make better decisions in my own life. My siblings had always managed to stay in touch even when they couldn't be around to make sure I didn't make the same mistakes they'd made. Now, here they were in person to support me. This was a day I was going to remember for the rest of my life, and not just because I was about to be drafted!

The morning of draft day, Kakie fixed me up like she always did whenever I had some important place to go. She was my hairstylist and fashion guru—my whole life, she'd always kept me in the hottest clothes and my hair laid whenever I needed it.

Once she finished doing my hair, I had to head to the ESPN campus. It was over there that they would do my makeup. After makeup I got dressed, and before showtime, our families came in and took pictures with us. My family was so excited and took tons of photos.

When my family left, Terri and Coach Brown stayed behind with me to watch the draft, which was airing on live TV.

Of all the players in that room, I was the last one

chosen: *"With the fourteenth pick, the Minnesota Lynx choose Sugar Rodgers of Georgetown University."* I got up, hugged both of my coaches, and went up to take a picture wearing a Lynx jersey.

My coaches were annoyed that I went so low in the draft, but I was just happy to get picked. I mean, I was a little upset too—fourteenth! But since I wore number fourteen for the Hoyas, and my mother passed away on July 14, I knew something good would come from all of this.

After doing a quick interview with the media, I was ready to see my family again and get something to eat. My phone was going crazy with all my friends and family members texting and calling.

When I got to the restaurant, my family members were all sitting there happily, smiling ear to ear

"You saved the family name, Auntie!" Kakie said, being her usual goofy self.

That night, all the pressure and the problems went away. I had never been so joyful in my life. My family made me even happier because of how excited they were for me. They showed me pictures from an Applebee's where people from my hometown had gathered to watch the draft. I felt proud that I'd brought everyone together, that I'd shown kids in my city that there was a way out of poverty no matter how many roadblocks you had to face.

The next day, I packed my bags and caught my flight

back to DC, where I would continue training. You see, even though I'd gotten drafted, that didn't mean I was on the team. I still had to go to training camp and actually make the team. I hated the thought of getting cut; I'd been cut from the USA World University Team and I did not want a repeat of that.

I trained in DC for a few days, and then I was off to Minnesota to start my WNBA career.

CHAPTER 28

MINNESOTA LYNX

THE TEAM ARRANGED FOR SOMEONE TO MEET ME at the Twin Cities airport and bring me to the hotel. After I checked in, one of the assistant coaches gave me a schedule of all the Lynx practices and various meetings and then showed me around the gym where I'd train. The team also rented a car for me to use.

I arrived early to the first day of training camp. I knew one of the girls on the team pretty well—Monica Wright—because she'd trained with me before the draft. I also knew a few others—one who'd gone to Georgetown, Rebekkah Brunson, and one more I'd played against in college, Maya Moore.

Training camp wasn't physically hard on me, but it was mentally rough. I found it difficult to memorize so many play sets in just a week. I knew my family would be calling to check in, so I asked them not to reach out too much unless there was an emergency. I had to stay intensely focused on training camp.

Luckily, Coach Brown and Coach Valentine had stayed on top of me, making sure I was in shape and mentally prepared. Basketball came naturally to me, but I always pushed myself and worked on the weakest parts of my game. I would work on a lot of ball-handling skills and creating my own shot. Everyone knew I could shoot the three ball, but ball-handling wasn't always my strongest skill.

A week into training camp, I pulled a muscle in my quad and had to stop running. I was sure they were going to cut me right then and there. The team trainer kept me out for a week. I spent that time icing my injury around the clock and doing the exercises they told me were safe. Plus, I hit up my doctor from Georgetown just to make sure everything I was doing was okay.

Once I was allowed to return to training, I was on my A game—making sure I knew all the plays and just keeping a positive attitude. I kept telling myself they would keep me because they knew what I was capable of.

A couple days later, they cut several players. It quickly became clear that the next cut would be either me or this other girl. I was hooping in training camp so I wasn't that worried, except for the fact that I'd missed the week because of my injury. I watched that day as the coaches walked over and cut the other girl and then came up to me and said, "Sugar, you made the team."

I was so happy deep down inside and I thanked them for the opportunity.

"You're not going to cry?" one of my coaches asked.

"I'm going to cry when I get to my room," I answered.

She laughed and said, "Congrats, Sugar, and welcome to the team. I'm looking forward to working with you."

Then everybody was all around congratulating me. I called my family and friends back home, letting them know that I'd made the team. And though I was overjoyed, I also knew in the back of my mind that I couldn't stop working hard. Now I had to figure how I was going to get some actual playing time with so many big names on the team.

My first official practice as a Minnesota Lynx went smoothly, though it was definitely tough, both physically and mentally. I knew this would be another big transition for me, because I had been the go-to player on the Hoyas for the past several years. Now *everybody* was a go-to player.

It didn't take me very long to settle in and adjust to the other players. I got to know my way around Minneapolis pretty quickly as well. But adjusting to the coaches was a different story, because being a professional athlete is all about business and politics. Sometimes it is not *what* you know, it's *who* you know.

I also learned quickly that the WNBA is a veterans' league and they favor the players who have the most experience, even if they're not always the best players on the team. So even if a young player has the skills, she might not always play.

CHAPTER 29

LIVING THE DREAM

ROOKIE YEAR WAS LIKE MY FRESHMAN YEAR of college, just on a different level. I had to work twice as hard as the next person in order to establish my game and name on the professional level. I was in the gym 24/7, getting my mind and body right.

Often, I would rewatch some of my college games, critiquing myself and identifying the parts of my game I needed to work on most. I treated my workouts like game situations. I arrived at the gym early and got shots up before practice, and always stayed afterward to get more shots up. I studied plays to make sure I was always in the right position.

In practice, we would often play against men; sometimes they were good players, other times they weren't, but they were always bigger, faster, and stronger. They gave us a run for our money, that's for sure.

Before an official WNBA scrimmage, we usually scrimmaged with the guys on the main court like a real game. I did pretty well and got to play a lot of minutes. Even though I felt like I was messing up, everybody kept telling me it was okay.

After preparing like crazy, it was now time for our official scrimmage against Connecticut at home. When it was my turn to sub into the game, I was nervous, naturally, but I reminded myself that it was just basketball—something I'd been doing most of my life.

My first shot was a three off the backboard for a buzzer beater. I played more minutes than I'd expected to, though I also knew the coaches like to include everyone in a scrimmage game so they can see where each player is as far as her skills and her ability to get the job done.

As the season went on, I found myself not playing many minutes. I was frustrated and I thought I deserved more playing time than I was getting. But I'd always known the team valued their veteran players. And there were some *great* veteran players, like Seimone Augustus and Lindsay Whalen. The Lynx had made it to the championship the previous year. We had players who'd been in the league five-plus years; they knew the system inside and out. Even though I was aware of all of this, however, sitting on the bench made me feel like I wasn't doing my job.

So I was frustrated, but I knew if I just continued to work hard every day and kept a clear head and clear heart, my turn would eventually come, whether it was this year or next. I had to be patient and wait my turn. I definitely didn't ever want people going around saying I wasn't working hard, or that I was complaining about my playing time, or that I had a bad attitude. I knew I needed to figure out how to help my team from the bench, so I focused on cheering them on when I wasn't on the court.

Even though I didn't play as much as I wanted to, I enjoyed my rookie year and ended up with a championship ring on my finger after we beat the Atlanta Dream in the Finals. I was learning so much it was almost impossible to take it all in.

The most important thing I learned that first year was what it takes to win a WNBA championship. The blood, sweat, and tears—all for a goal you set to accomplish from the very beginning. All of this makes winning a championship that much sweeter in the end.

CHAPTER 30

DREAM BIG

I LOVE PLAYING BASKETBALL, but it wasn't always my dream. I mean, close your eyes and imagine doing something you love and getting paid for it. I hadn't always imagined that could be my reality. But look at me now, I've been getting paid for playing basketball in the WNBA for eight years! It's something I'm dedicated to, inspired by, and passionate about. If I didn't get paid, I would still play because it makes me happy. At the end of the day, your mental well-being is what counts—as the saying goes, money can't buy you happiness.

As soon as I realized that playing ball was going to be my *profession,* I knew I had to give it my all to overcome the obstacles in my way. Obstacles can be extremely daunting, but they can also be overcome. Some will be tougher than others, but I honestly believe that almost nothing is impossible. Even if you *think* something is impossible, at least try before quitting. You might fail, but at least you committed yourself to it.

And all of us have different types of obstacles.

Middle-class, suburban children might be more used to two-parent households, siblings in college, the luxury of material items, and simply more opportunities; whereas children living in poverty are more often accustomed to single-parent households, drug abuse, physical abuse, some type of government assistance, and maybe a family member who's been in and out of jail. Sometimes it's hard to see past that, if it's all you know. But trust me, it doesn't have to be your life.

CHAPTER 31

SELF-TALK AND POSITIVITY

WHAT IS "SELF-TALK"? It's hard to explain the conversations I have with myself, but I start off every day with a positive reflection, such as, *Dang, girl, you're doing good!* Some might say I am my own biggest fan, but I feel like more than a fan—I'm my own *motivator*. When times get hard, when I'm stressed or overwhelmed, it's up to *me* to figure out how to comfort myself. And while I've always been close to my family, I believe wholeheartedly in the saying that you are born alone and die alone. I feel as if no one else can truly understand the adversities or struggles that I have gone through because everyone's way of dealing with any situation is unique.

I have learned to be alone from the loss of my mother and father, and from the separation in age from my siblings, as well as their time in prison. In a way, sometimes I feel like an only child, and because of that I've spent a lot of time with my own thoughts. Being alone with your thoughts can be dangerous, but it can also be uplifting. Sometimes I'll go negative and doubt myself, but other times I'll say, *Self, why are you whining? You know you're the best in your league!*

Some people think that if you talk to yourself, you're crazy. Well, if that's true, then I'm a lunatic, because I spend plenty of time chatting with myself. Self-talk is where I get to know my true self; it also helps me envision what I need to do next.

Over the years, I've spent a lot of time comparing my life to others'. I've often wondered, *Why are all these crazy things happening to ME?* As a young girl, I didn't have much control over a lot of things. Growing up in the hood, I didn't have any assurances of where I would end up. I took a lot of gambles not really knowing what the outcome would be.

I wanted that "American Dream" that you often see in movies—the white picket fence, kids running around in the front yard, two parents watching from the porch. Yet I learned at an early age that I had to face reality. I had to learn how to accept my perfectly imperfect family, because nobody's flawless. Most importantly, I realized that I *did* have that American Dream, even if it didn't resemble the Hollywood version. Plus, I learned that even when things look good from the outside, you never know what's really going on with other people.

Although most of us seek support and encouragement from others, sometimes that support will fade. Not because people are betraying you, but because the truth is, people will always focus most on their own lives. That's why you must have faith in your dreams.

So here's when I take my thoughts to boot camp. There's always a time to rev the engine and get ready at the starting line. But to keep constant faith in your own dreams, you have to act on them *daily*. In my mind, I've always had a blueprint for how my life should go.

My first goal was to develop strategies for getting out of the hood; the next goal was to live through my talents. So I said, *Self, how will you manage to do these things?* You have to align your actions with your goals. It wouldn't have made sense to tell myself I wanted to be a basketball player while I was just taking golf lessons, or to think that I could leave the hood without going to school or saving money.

So even when I wanted to give up, I coached my own thoughts; sometimes I was harder on myself than any coach, teacher, or mentor could ever be. I was definitely brutally honest, and sometimes I couldn't stand what I had to say to myself! There were other times when I let myself off the hook instead of holding myself accountable for my actions. But hey, that's one perk of being your own best friend. And if there is one person who will never let me down, it's me. I can depend on myself to plan, strategize, motivate, and celebrate *me*!

Now that I've achieved my goal of getting out of the hood and living through my talents, it's time to conquer a new one. Existence is forever taking shape, and if you're not growing in new areas or expanding, then you're not really living.

My current goal is to share my story with others, hoping that people can relate to and learn from my experiences. There are pros and cons to exposing yourself, but I prefer to focus on the positive outcomes of doing this.

I had always wanted to give back to my community because I knew what it was like to grow up surrounded by people not succeeding. As my professional career has progressed, I've spent a lot of my time giving back. Most people give back by donating money. I give back by talking to teenagers and adults in schools and communities—giving them guidance on how to stay on the right track. Through sharing my stories of struggle, I hope others can relate to me and learn something. I want to open their eyes to a bigger picture so they can stop settling for less.

Instead of gangbanging and repping your hood, represent a college. Instead of selling drugs, start your own business, even if it's just mowing people's lawns. Instead of sinking into despair about all the violence you see, look beyond that and give somebody a helping hand.

Despite all of my self-talk and the skills I've developed to rely on myself, dependency on others is also a common narrative to survival. We all depend on others, whether it be our families, people in our communities, our friends, etc. But as you grow, it's important to make sure your circle includes optimists.

I always advise people to watch the company you keep. If you want to succeed, surround yourself with positive people and become a chameleon of sorts, taking on their positivity. It's easy to spot a negative person right away because he or she will often throw shade on your dreams or the decisions you make. Positivity is infectious, and the more optimistic people you have around you, the better. You want individuals who have your best interests at heart—meaning, they will tell you like it is the entire time, even if the truth sometimes hurts.

I think it's important to take advice from those people who have been there and done that. Additionally, it's important to network with people who are already where you would like to be in life. Taking advice from someone who has experienced a difficult path can help you to avoid making the same mistakes. The advice I've gotten over the years has shaped me immensely.

You also have to take constructive criticism; you need to be able to embrace the good with the bad. It's all good news in one way or another; it's just how you look at it. Believe me, I know how hard it is to hear about what areas in my life I need to improve upon. But another way to look at this is that someone thinks you are good enough to correct.

As we get older, who we depend on changes. You have to create a circle of folks who will support you *no matter what.*

My personal education has been one of knowledge gained from a never-ending list of people and life experiences. I cannot dismiss any of the impact that these interactions have had on me. They have all participated equally in creating my success. The positive people in my life and the negative ones—any way you look at it, they were all good for me. My haters are my motivators and my supporters are my lifeline.

Acknowledgments

First and foremost, I want to thank God—without Him, none of this would be possible.

I would love to thank my friends and family: my sister Sharon Rodgers, her daughter Ebony, her two sons, Vanshawn and Keshawn, may his soul rest in peace, and my brother DeShawn Rodgers, who introduced me to sports. And, oh yeah, I want to thank ALL of my nieces and nephews!

Thank you as well to Kenya Latham for sharing his mother, and to Rickeda Fofana and her husband, who helped raise me. I cannot forget about my cousin Melissa Carrol and the fun times we had at Aunt Linda's house.

Many thanks to former WNBA superstar Swin Cash for introducing me to Akashic Books.

Special shout-out to my best friends: Ransheda Jennings, Trinese Fox, and Jalisa Morgan.

I want to thank everyone else who had a positive impact on my life. If you helped me along the way, thank you! I would not be the woman I am today if it was not for you all. I love you!